CW00640896

THE BEST OF WORDS OF LIFE

'All Scripture is God-breathed and is useful for teaching, rebuking, correcting and training in righteousness, so that the man of God may be thoroughly equipped for every good work.'
(2 Timothy 3:16,17, NIV)

The Best of Words of Life

Meeting God Through the Bible

Compiled and edited by William Clark

Hodder & Stoughton

LONDON SYDNEY AUCKLAND

and

The Salvation Army

Scripture quotations taken from the HOLY BIBLE,
NEW INTERNATIONAL VERSION, copyright © 1973,
1978, 1984 by International Bible Society, are used
by permission of Hodder & Stoughton Ltd, a member of
the Hodder Headline Plc Group. All rights reserved.

Scripture quotations from the New English Bible (NEB)
are used by permission of the Oxford University Press
and the Cambridge University Press 1961, 1970; and from
the Good News Bible (GNB) and the Revised Standard
Version (RSV) by permission of Harper Collins Religious,
a division of HarperCollins Publishers Limited.

Copyright © 1998 The Salvation Army

First published in Great Britain 1998

The right of The Salvation Army to be identified
as the Author of the Work has been asserted by them
in accordance with the Copyright, Designs and Patents
Act 1988.

10 9 8 7 6 5 4 3 2 1

All rights reserved. No part of this publication may
be reproduced, stored in a retrieval system, or transmitted,
in any form or by any means without the prior written
permission of the publisher, nor be otherwise circulated
in any form of binding or cover other than that in which
it is published and without a similar condition being
imposed on the subsequent purchaser.

British Library Cataloguing in Publication Data
A record for this book is available from the British Library.

ISBN 0 340 71418 2

Typeset by Hewer Text Ltd, Edinburgh
Printed and bound in Great Britain by
Mackays of Chatham PLC, Chatham, Kent

Hodder and Stoughton
A Division of Hodder Headline PLC
338 Euston Road
London NW1 3BH

CONTENTS

THE BEST OF WORDS OF LIFE

ABBREVIATIONS USED
FOR BIBLE VERSIONS

AV	Authorised (King James) Version
GNB	Good News Bible
JB	Jerusalem Bible
JBP	J.B. Phillips's Translation
JM	James Moffatt's Translation
LB	Living Bible – Kenneth Taylor
NEB	New English Bible
NIV	New International Version
RSV	Revised Standard Version
WB	William Barclay's Translation

INTRODUCTION

In 1955 The Salvation Army began to publish, principally for its own members, a series of Bible study notes with the title *The Soldier's Armoury*. Though the Army had from its earliest days provided books, newspapers, magazines galore to equip its soldiers for 'the good fight', these notes were a new venture and an instant success.

Then, in 1968, *The Soldier's Armoury* appeared in a new, enlarged format as a joint publication with Hodder and Stoughton. The channels of distribution were now much wider and the circulation increased considerably. Christians of many denominations began to use the notes, which received high praise from well-known Christian leaders and writers.

William Barclay wrote that *The Soldier's Armoury* 'is everything such a book should be . . . it deserves the widest possible public'. J.B. Phillips said he considered the book provided 'the sort of help people need in reading the Bible'. Others commented in similarly warm and approving terms.

In 1989 the title was changed. *The Soldier's Armoury* became *Words of Life*. The book was redesigned to give it a more modern image and, instead of coming out twice a year, it was issued – and still is – in four-monthly volumes. But the basic approach remained as at the beginning. A respect for biblical scholarship is combined with a warm devotional tone closely related to everyday life. The authors and the format may change, but God's word in the Bible is unchanging – and remains relevant.

Compiler and publishers are confident that this selection of 'the best of' will be warmly welcomed both by present readers of the notes and also by others who, taking up this volume, may decide

1

the contents suit them, and be encouraged to become regular readers as the notes are published.

The comments are here organised into nine sections, each with a major theme, and have been drawn from the work of previous writers as well as from that of the current one. No attempt has been made to identify writers with particular comments: all were one in their prayer that the truth, inspiration and challenge contained in the divine word would, through *their* words, flow out to their readers.

The high standards set by the first writers, Harry Dean and Fred Brown, were maintained through the years by Bernard Mobbs, William Clark, John Coutts, Clifford Ashworth, Clifford Kew, Kenneth Lawson, David Dalziel and now by Harry Read. They are asked to accept this word of sincere appreciation.

Part 1

WHAT JESUS SAID

Jesus was a superb teacher. In the main he conveyed his message, particularly as recorded in the first three Gospels, by stories – parables – basing them on homely, everyday situations. He talked about sheep wandering away and getting lost; about a headstrong young man leaving home to make his own way in the world, and making a mess of things; about a farmer sowing his seed – and so on. The people could, in one way or another, identify with all that. Such incidents had happened to them, in their family or to the family living down the street. So they listened and they understood.

But if his teaching was given in simple terms, the themes were large and profound: the Kingdom (or rule) of God, the Fatherhood of God, the sad consequences of sin, the attitudes in life that make for true happiness, and much more. And, we are told, 'the common people heard him gladly (Mark 12:37).

When we turn to John's Gospel, however, we 'breathe a different atmosphere', as J.B. Phillips puts it. We could almost think that here we have a different Jesus. The Jesus of John doesn't speak in parables, but in long and sometimes involved discourses, with a style very different from that of the other Gospels. All this, with other differences, has given rise to a great deal of scholarly discussion.

But Jesus would not have spoken in different ways at different times. And there is only one Jesus. It must be that John, acquainted with the other Gospels set out, not to cover their ground again, but to present a commentary on, an interpretation of, what Jesus had said. He was writing for a different constituency and at a later time. And as to the special spiritual value of John's account there can be no doubt at all.

But we need Matthew, Mark and Luke also. The Holy Spirit

3

obviously felt so! Luke and Matthew built on what Mark had earlier written and John complements them. Taking them together we have teaching of incalculable and timeless significance.

The comments that follow are based on passages from all four Gospels.

THE BLISS OF TOTAL DEPENDENCE

MATTHEW 5:1–3 – 'Blessed are the poor in spirit, for theirs is the kingdom of heaven' (v. 3, RSV).

There is a poverty of spirit which describes the sad reality of people who are ungenerous and unthankful. They may or may not be well endowed with material things, but they diminish other people and, without realising it, diminish themselves in the process. Of people marked by that kind of poverty our Lord had nothing but hard words.

However, there is a poverty of spirit which meets with his full approval. Such poverty has nothing to do with deprivation, or low feelings of self-worth, but everything to do with a strong experience of forgiveness, and the indwelling of the Holy Spirit.

This poverty of spirit is born in honesty when we realise that in our own strength we cannot meet the high standards which God requires of us, nor provide ourselves with the satisfactions our hearts demand. We therefore confess our inadequacy, turning to God in our need and we find he graciously handles our weaknesses, making his own tremendous resources available to us.

It is as we learn to lean upon God completely, progressively learning the secrets of self denial and dependence, that we become poor in spirit and inheritors of the kingdom of our Lord.

Such poverty is marked by joy and peace. Material things are held in a wise perspective and there is a progressive bonding with our Lord, whose life and energy have become ours.

> *Come and rejoice with me;*
> *I, once so sick at heart,*
> *Have met with one who knows my case,*
> *And knows the healing art.*
> *Elizabeth Rundle-Charles*

A CHRISTIAN'S INFLUENCE

MATTHEW 5:13–16 – 'You are the salt of the earth . . . You are the light of the world' (vv. 13,14, NIV).

What an amazing thing! Jesus told a little group of humble Jewish fishermen living in a remote corner of the mighty Roman Empire that they were to be the 'salt of the earth' and the 'light of the world'. Yet this was both their privilege and responsibility. That privilege and that responsibility have never been withdrawn from the charter of Christian discipleship. Both metaphors speak of the Christian's influence in the world, influence by both *preservation* and *revelation*.

Salt saves from putrefaction and insipidity, and the effect of Christianity in today's confused and despairing world, and of the prayers, faith and zeal of Christian people, cannot be assessed. However, Jesus allowed for the sad possibility of some Christians failing in their duty, as he reminded his disciples of the possibility of the salt becoming insipid. A sobering thought!

By his use of the word 'light' Jesus showed the Christian's responsibility to reveal God to others – note *God* and not the Christian himself. As a lamp does not draw attention to itself but to whatever else is in the room, so the Christian brings the focus and praise to God.

Every Christian, then, should be an example of purity (salt purifies) and of radiant living (for salt brings flavour and character to food) and so makes it easier for others to believe in a good God and to live good lives. It was said of William Pitt that no one went into his presence who did not come out a better person.

These parables remind us that Christians cannot withdraw from the world. Nor can they conceal from the world where their loyalty lies and what the inspiration of their lives is. This, too, is a challenging thought.

PERFECTION

MATTHEW 5:43–48 – 'You, therefore, must be perfect as
your heavenly Father is perfect' (v. 48, RSV).

The idea of Christian perfection causes much anxiety. Over-
emphasising the need to be perfect can take us very close to
Old Testament attempts to keep the Law. We want a standard
by which to measure our perfection or lack of it. The easiest
standard to take is some standard of visible conduct. I am good
because I have done this particular thing, or because I act in this
way or that.

But Jesus shows, over and over again, that coming up to certain
standards of behaviour is no way to judge perfection. We need
only to look at the story of the Pharisee and the publican (Luke
18:10–14) to see that.

Christian perfection will express itself in action, but it is the
immeasurable action of loving one's enemy – and that will usually
be misunderstood as weakness or as folly.

It may help us to consider how God's perfection was expressed
in Jesus. First, he came as a baby. There was no immediate physical
perfection. He learnt to walk, talk, feed himself in the way any
ordinary person does.

Then he became an adolescent. He faced the same traumas we
all face, and made similar mistakes to the rest of us – like sending
his parents silly with worry when he stayed back at the Temple in
Jerusalem instead of going home (Luke 2:41–52). Third, he had
fully human emotions as an adult. Jesus was happy, sad, angry
with people, just like the rest of us.

His perfection lay in his complete commitment to his Father's
will and his struggle to understand that will. Retain that idea
uppermost and we will not stray far from the path followed by
the great example of Jesus himself. It is in that way that we reach
the Father's perfection – by relating to, and accepting commitment
to Jesus.

ACTS OF RIGHTEOUSNESS

MATTHEW 6:5–8 – 'When you pray, do not be like the hypocrites, for they love to pray standing in the synagogues and on the street corners to be seen by men' (v. 5, NIV).

Apparently, a familiar sight in Jerusalem was of those who deliberately displayed their piety in order to be known as pious people. It seems strange that prayer, which is meant to express a personal obligation to and relationship with God, can be used for this unworthy purpose, and yet experience confirms that this is an ever-new problem.

Prayers to impress people rather than God display spiritual immaturity. William Law, in his *Serious Call to a Devout and Holy Life* said, 'Let a man, when he is most delighted with his own figure ... contemplate our Blessed Lord ... nailed upon a cross; and then let him consider how absurd it must be, for a heart full of pride and vanity to pray to God through the sufferings of such a meek and crucified Saviour.'

Such prayers are pointless anyway. Not many people are fooled and God is certainly not deceived. We know instinctively when a prayer has made us aware of the reality of God, or when someone is merely using words.

An old lady who attended Carr's Lane Church, Birmingham, said of the minister, Dr R.W. Dale, 'Ah me! I cannot understand his sermons but his prayers do me so much good that I always come.'

It was the same minister who earlier had written, 'When we pray, our great design is not to move men, but to move God.' When prayer moves God, it moves us also. Those who pray to move people have also received their reward in full.

> *Lord, when I come to thee in prayer,*
> *With modest words, though bold,*
> *I would of thee be more aware,*
> *And by thee be controlled.*
>
> *Anon*

BEWILDERED AND DEJECTED

MATTHEW 9:35–38 – 'When he saw the crowds, he had compassion on them, because they were harassed and helpless, like sheep without a shepherd' (v. 36, NIV).

The first verse of this reading indicates that Jesus carried out a more widespread ministry than is suggested by the ten miracles recorded in the verses from 8:1 to 9:34. The evangelist has here to be content with giving a brief summary, but we should notice that it was a ministry of teaching, healing and 'preaching the good news of the kingdom'.

Jesus saw the depth and the extent of the needs of the people. Their situation cried out for leadership, care and nurture. The good news of the kingdom offered hope, and there was a rich harvest for the reaping. Jesus was limited to the laws of time and space, and he recognised that the task was too vast for one man; others must be involved in the work.

The twelve disciples were soon to be chosen (recorded in chapter 10) and given their responsibilities, but notice that in verse 38 there is an indication that even so the great mission will require many more. Christ's prayer is that such workers will be found and sent out.

Viewing the world today we Christians are often bewildered by the enormity of the need. We have a conviction that men and women can find hope in Christ but the challenge seems so vast. What can we do? How can we reach them? We can pray for workers, and we can begin to answer that prayer by making *ourselves* available for the work of the kingdom – and doing it today!

RECEIVING THE GOOD SEED

MATTHEW 13:1–9 – 'He who has ears, let him hear' (v. 9, NIV).

A sower working in the fields would have been a very familiar sight in the days of Jesus, so the parable which occupies the major part of this reading would not appear very remarkable to his hearers. The ordinary listener could easily dismiss it as something of little consequence, but the final words suggest that there is more in it than the casual listener might suspect.

It has been suggested that the traditional title given to this parable, the parable of the sower, is misleading. It should be called the parable of *the soils*. No stress is placed on the skill of the sower or the quantity of the seed; the emphasis is all on the nature of the soil. An interpretation is provided in the chapter later on, but it is obvious that here fruitfulness, or lack of it, is what is being highlighted.

Much of what has gone before in this Gospel shows that people received Jesus's word of the Kingdom in ways that varied from stony rejection to ready enthusiasm. It was the wise who received the word (cf. 11:19) and brought forth the harvest.

The parable is a timely word for us as we receive God's word through Jesus. It is also a reminder that as we scatter the seed of the gospel, its fruitfulness depends on those who receive it. A verse John Masefield wrote at the end of the Second World War might be applied to our Christian responsibility to *keep on sowing*:

> *After destruction, lo, a human need,*
> *For folly, knowledge, and for blindness, sight.*
> *Our harvests, who shall reckon? We sow seed*
> *That unborn generations may have light.*

SMALL BEGINNINGS

MATTHEW 13:31–32 – 'The Kingdom of Heaven is like . . .
a mustard seed . . . the smallest of all seeds' (GNB).

Jesus's listeners might have thought he was making an exaggerated claim when he told this parable. He had gathered around him only a few followers who, judged by worldly standards, showed little promise as pioneers of a movement symbolised by a tree so big 'that birds come and nest in its branches'.

When Jesus left the earth there seemed little to show for his work – a small company of men and women with little influence or learning between them. Small beginnings indeed! But the movement had life and it would grow, as Jesus said. The Christian Church is probably the only institution that has survived these two thousand years.

We should not underestimate small beginnings. What has been proved true of the Kingdom of God (of which, we should remember, the Church is but an instrument) may be true of our own personal progress in the life of faith and holiness. While on occasions Jesus rebuked the disciples for the smallness of their faith, he also said that if they had faith, faith no bigger than a mustard seed, they could move mountains (Matthew 17:20).

Yet the small faith of the believer, while in itself valid and valuable, may grow. We may feel we are among those of little faith and therefore of little account. It's not true! There is potential stored within us of which God himself is aware. We, too, may develop as we learn of Christ.

UNSPECTACULAR GROWTH

MATTHEW 13:33 – 'The Kingdom of Heaven is like yeast'
(GNB).

This parable, like that of the mustard seed (vv. 31,32), has to do with the growth of the Kingdom of God (or, as Matthew prefers, the Kingdom of Heaven). In both parables the end is shown to be out of all proportion to the beginning. While in the mustard seed parable the emphasis is on the extent of the growth of the Kingdom, here it falls on the method of the growth.

About yeast it has been said, 'It influences the particle nearest it, and so its work spreads until a tumultuous upheaval takes place and all is leavened.' Applying this to the influence of the believer brings an inescapable challenge: how truly do we influence for Christ those nearest to us? It is easy for us to be dazzled by spectacular Christian service; it may also make us complacent. There may be legitimate reasons – family responsibilities, for instance – why we cannot tackle the great and the heroic, and it might be thought that therefore we are absolved from responsibility for taking any action in the cause of Christ. The truth is that the work of the Kingdom has to be done most often in unspectacular ways.

Though there are times when it is our duty to *do* and to *speak*, and when inactivity and silence are cowardly capitulation, the yeast speaks of a life *lived* quietly for Christ *in the everyday*. A Christian man was asked, 'Under whose preaching were you converted?' and he replied, 'Under nobody's preaching; under my aunt's living.'

Wrote Dr Jowett, 'Do not let us think we need to be stars in order to shine. It was by the ministry of a candle that a woman found her lost piece of silver.'

NEW TREASURES

MATTHEW 13:51,52 – 'Every teacher of the Law who becomes a disciple in the Kingdom of heaven is like the owner of a house who takes new and old things out of his storeroom' (v. 52, GNB).

At the conclusion of this teaching in parables, Jesus asks his disciples if they have understood what he has been saying. On receiving a reply in the affirmative, he uses yet another parable to sum up the significance of what they have learned.

This parable stresses that Christian teaching did not require the abandonment of what was good and true in their former understanding, but that the acquisition of new truth enhanced the usefulness of the old. It also extended the usefulness of the teacher. In their ministry the disciples, who were drawn mainly from working class occupations but who would have a basic knowledge of the Law, could use what they had learned from Jesus to give their preaching its unique Christian emphasis.

This truth is significant for twentieth-century Christians. Christian witness takes place in the contemporary world where the followers of Jesus have to cope with the demands of industry, commerce and the professions. In such circumstances it is impossible to dispense with the skills and knowledge our daily work requires.

The Christian also has the responsibility to reject or correct what is evil as well as to cultivate what is good. The unique Christian contribution which can be made is to take what we have learned of Christ into every aspect of life. Then we have new treasures as well as old in our storehouse, and we can make the whole available to others.

NO EASY WAY TO FORGIVENESS

MATTHEW 18:23–25 – 'Forgive your brother from your heart' (v. 35, NIV).

Jesus told this striking story to answer Peter's question about how many times he should forgive one who had wronged him (vv. 21,22). It is made clear that forgiveness is not a matter on which it can be calculated how many times or under what conditions it should be granted. The only rule about forgiveness is that there are no rules! This does not conflict with Jesus's teaching that God forgives us as we forgive (Matthew 6:14,15).

What Jesus said there is true, of course, but not in the sense that God's forgiveness of us is dependent on our forgiveness of others. If God cannot forgive us it is not because he is unwilling, but because we, by our refusal to offer forgiveness, become incapable of receiving it. It is only our own willingness to forgive that makes possible a saving relationship between God and us. Similarly, only on our willingness to forgive are enriching relationships made possible between us and our fellows.

What wonderful things forgiveness may do in human relationships, yet how reluctant we are to exercise it. We appear more concerned about our hurt pride, about making it clear we were the offended-against and not the offender, and even about 'turning the tables', than about forgiveness. Even in the closest relationships – between husband and wife, for instance – such attitudes are possible.

True forgiveness does not ask for the wrong to be redressed, nor demand apologies; it lacks self-interest and condescension. True forgiveness is free and unstinting. An impossible standard? Recollection of the immensity of our debt to others, and especially to God, will help us to see how *just*, if not how *easy*, it really is.

FACING FACTS ABOUT OURSELVES

MATTHEW 25:14–30 – 'He gave one five thousand pounds, another two thousand and another one thousand – according to the man's ability' (v. 15, JBP).

It is the responsibility of all Christians to learn to accept other people as they are, with their foibles and limitations. It is no less important that they learn to accept themselves. That means all of us! Of course, self-acceptance may be nothing more than laziness; unwillingness to make an effort at effecting a remedy in circumstances, character and conduct. When improvements can be made it is plainly our duty to make them.

But where there are personal limitations about which nothing can be done, the fact should be honestly faced. When we realise that our youthful dreams are not going to materialise, it is of little use our sitting down to lament the way life has treated us. We have to accept the situation as it is and do with it what we may.

Too often people who feel they have 'missed out' in some way fail to take advantage of what they have, which may be considerably more than, in their self-pity, they have realised. The one-talent man in Jesus's parable is true to life. He mistrusted himself, developed an inferiority complex, and did nothing at all with what he did have. This is the trap in which one-talent people are often caught.

Wrote William Barclay, 'God never demands from a man abilities which he has not got: but God does demand from a man that he should use to the full the abilities he does possess. Men are not equal in talent: but men can be equal in effort.' For our encouragement (are not most of us just ordinary folk?) Jesus taught that we shall not be blamed for having only one talent, but we shall be judged by how we use it.

NO MAN AN ISLAND

MARK 2:1–12 – 'When Jesus saw their faith, he said to the paralysed man, "My son, your sins are forgiven"' (v. 5, NEB).

There is nothing like reading the Gospels for shattering our over-simplified theological formulas. Judging by most doctrinal statements the assurance of forgiveness should have been given when Jesus, looking at the paralysed man, saw *his* faith. But no, it was when he saw the expectant trust of the ingenious friends, who dismantled part of the roof to lower the sufferer to Christ's feet, that the Master said, 'My son, your sins *are* forgiven.'

The scribes were shocked by this apparent blasphemy. Who can forgive sins but God? Perhaps *we* could be shocked by this contradiction of religious individualism. Who can have his sins forgiven, we say, except he who has personal faith?

The facts of life line up with the Bible to undermine our too tidy picture of 'God-and-my-soul'. What is it keeps the member of Alcoholics Anonymous off the bottle – his own faith or the faith of the group? What has made possible the transformation of some of the lowest of society in the history of The Salvation Army – their own faith or the faith of the Salvationists who surrounded the new converts with affection and concern? The answer to each question is – both!

When we make faith only an individual matter we conveniently escape responsibility for the failures around us, and pride ourselves on our own trust. Has personal faith brought us the assurance of salvation? Good. Has it ever created an environment in which another has heard the word of grace?

LORD OF THE SABBATH

MARK 2:23–28 – 'The Sabbath was made for the good of man; man was not made for the Sabbath' (v. 27, GNB).

The Sabbath, says the Talmud (the body of Jewish Law), is a delight, the most frequent Jewish Festival, celebrating God's work of creation, a day of recreation which all should be able to share. To make this possible there must be differences between the Sabbath and other days. Christians often try to achieve this for *their* Sabbath (Sunday) by legislation, but when this happens the delight runs the risk of becoming a burden. Rules accepted by one generation become burdensome to the next.

Achieving a balance between rest and recreational activity is not easy. If people are to enjoy organised recreation someone has to organise it – and so their Sunday loses some of its significance.

Essential services must be kept going. We need water on Sunday. Without electricity cities would grind to a halt; fridges and freezers would heat up, disease would spread. Without some people being prepared to undertake essential services on Sunday we would all suffer. But where can we draw the line between what is essential and what is not? It is a problem to which there is no ready answer. The Pharisees in our Lord's day found an answer by producing many complicated laws. Others in our own day completely disregard Sunday. Both extremes are unsatisfactory.

Yet again we are driven to follow our Lord's example. We must use Sunday in the most beneficial way we can. It was made for us, so we should use it. If we can rest, then we should rest. If we must work, we should let our work enable others to rest. And we should take every opportunity for worship, praising God for *that* privilege, which can make Sunday, like the Sabbath, a delight.

PROMISE AND WARNING

MARK 3:20–30 – 'No sin, no slander, is beyond forgiveness for men; but whoever slanders the Holy Spirit can never be forgiven' (vv. 28,29, NEB).

The crude incomprehension of his ministry by the people who said, 'He must be mad!' must have wounded Christ; yet there was a brutal straightforwardness about this reaction. It remained for the religious authorities, as so often in history, to commit the really heinous sin. Confronted with a man who fitted none of their preconceived categories they deviously attributed his works of mercy to the devil. This, said Jesus, was unpardonable.

In Matthew's version of the same incident Jesus says that speaking against the Son of Man may be forgiven, but not blasphemy against the Holy Spirit. The former sin, as Bede Griffith has pointed out, often means to reject Christ 'as he is known to weak and fallible men often in a distorted and unworthy form'. To sin against the Holy Spirit, however, is to reject the light that is given to every man. It is to change the light that is within us to darkness. Probably Jesus was speaking of a persistent rejection rather than any one act or word.

Bunyan, Cowper, and many others have been haunted by the fear that they have committed the unforgivable sin. However, those most troubled are the least likely to be guilty. The morbid mind typically misses the glorious promise which is linked with this solemn warning: 'All men's sins can be forgiven and all their blasphemies.' All? This comprehensiveness is more astounding than the one solitary exception.

THE URGENT CALL TO DISCIPLESHIP

LUKE 10:1–16 – 'The harvest is plentiful, but the workers are few. Ask the Lord of the harvest, therefore, to send out workers into his harvest field' (vv. 2,3, NIV).

Jesus's instructions to the group of seventy-two disciples emphasised the urgency of the mission that was theirs. They were to take no unnecessary burdens and to allow no unnecessary distractions on the way (v. 4). They were not to be governed by thoughts of personal comfort – looking for better accommodation – and neither by matters of lesser importance, such as the ritual cleanliness of the food they were offered (v. 7). The disciples' task was to announce the Kingdom of God by both word and deed, and to the fulfilment of that task all else had to give way.

If we lose the sense of urgency about the proclamation of the Kingdom then our gospel will be the poorer. It is not that the spirit of our work is determined by whether or not we think the end of all things is imminent; irrespective of that the message is urgent because the Kingdom of God is already a reality since Jesus has come to our world.

Yes, the time *has* come! The harvest can be gathered! Let there therefore be no delay. Why should a soul wait one moment longer than necessary before discovering the Kingdom of God for himself?

Thus we can understand better the Lord's injunction for us to pray that God will send more labourers to harvest the crop that is ready. But we should note that whoever prays that prayer will feel bound to respond by offering himself, herself, for the work. When a man or a woman prays for labourers, the Lord replies, 'Be on your way.'

THE BOUNDARIES OF COMPASSION

LUKE 10:25–37 – 'A Samaritan . . . took pity on him. He bandaged his wounds, pouring on oil and wine . . . brought him to an inn and took care of him' (vv. 33,34, NIV).

The theologian wanted to delineate how far the good man must go: 'What must I do to inherit eternal life' (v. 25); 'Who is my neighbour?' (v. 29). Jesus's parable showed that compassion which is concerned with how soon it can 'draw the line' is not genuine. Not only did the Samaritan make the only right response, it was a wholehearted response, placing himself in danger, using the first-aid kit he might need himself, getting his good clothes dirty, using Shanks's pony instead of a Samaritan donkey, doing without sleep, paying out good money. We might think it was all a bit much!

Some of us spend all our time discussing who might be helped and how, while others are out there helping them! Jesus challenges us to extend rather than limit the outreach of compassion. Of course, there are limits to what any one person can do. We may spread our activities so widely that they have no depth, or drain our physical resources beyond the point of no return.

A professor concerned with preparing students for the ministry advised them not to visit more than two bereaved families a day: 'It should take so much out of you, emotionally and spiritually, that you will not be able to do a third time.' The Samaritan *did* hand the case over to the doctor at the cottage hospital, though at his own expense. There *are* limits; but good Samaritans must bear responsibility even if they do not do all the work themselves.

FEAR AND FAVOUR

LUKE 12:1–7 – 'Fear him who, after the killing of the body, has power to throw you into hell . . . the very hairs of your head are all numbered' (vv. 5,7, NIV).

The two statements above reveal a strong contrast in the character of God, but even human beings do not react in the same way in every situation. If they did it would be a sign of weakness not goodness. How can we expect, then, an infinite God to make the same reaction to everyone, regardless of their response to him? Some see condemnation on his face, others see love.

So Jesus says that physical death is insignificant compared to the destiny of the soul. The fact that so many people fear the first but ignore the second surely reveals a lack, characteristic of our age, of a serious belief in an afterlife. In contrast, Francis Lyte, visiting a dying friend who had always had a vivid realisation of the Lord's presence and grace, found him repeating, 'O abide with me! Abide with me!' – words used by Lyte years later in his famous hymn.

The faithless person, then, may regard physical death as a cruel and fearsome fate, because he cannot see it as a birth into a much better life beyond. Similarly, the world regards hell, if it believes in it at all, as a cruel invention of a sadistic God. The fact is that the God who is love *has* to make a stand against sin for the sake of his creatures, but he has provided a way by which all may be saved. If God had his way hell would be empty!

PREOCCUPATION WITH THE TRIVIAL

JOHN 4:1–15 – 'The Samaritan woman said to him, "You are a Jew and I am a Samaritan woman. How can you ask me for a drink? . . . you have nothing to draw with and the well is deep . . . Sir, give me this water so that I won't get thirsty"' (vv. 9,11,15, NIV).

To the Samaritan woman Jesus was at first just a man who was prepared to instal piped-in water for her in exchange for a drink from the well! Can we scoff at her foolishness when so many of us are taken in by bargain offers only slightly more credible? Can we judge her when we so often assess spiritual situations by material criteria?

She was sensible enough to see two snags and honest enough to air them. She didn't see *why* Jesus *should* have dealings with her and she didn't see *how* he *could* make good his side of the deal. Why *should* he, a Jew, demean himself by opening a conversation with a Samaritan, and a woman at that (v. 9)? Surely there must be more in it for him than a drink of water? Then, how *could* he give her 'living' water in return if he had no equipment – no bucket, no rope (v. 11)? *Could* he deliver the goods?

Jesus tried to explain his offer more clearly, speaking of water that eliminates thirst, of an 'inner spring' of 'eternal life' (v. 14). Nevertheless, like many a doorstep purchaser, though she didn't understand the technical jargon, she took the offer just the same. Then she immediately showed she didn't understand the product by saying it would save her work, because she wouldn't have to collect water from the well any more (v. 15).

It's rather like someone getting rid of the bath because they had bought a washing machine! Ridiculous, but don't we often trivialise and materialise God's offers to us almost as foolishly?

UPLIFTING CHRIST

JOHN 12:20–36 – 'But I, when I am lifted up, will draw all men to myself' (v. 32, NIV).

There were those present on this occasion who knew that being 'lifted up' was a reference to crucifixion. Quite naturally they failed to see how the Messiah could die (v. 32), and especially to die by such shameful means, hence their question, 'How can you say "The Son of Man must be lifted up?"'. However, the lifting up of Jesus was also part of his exaltation. To both the Son and Father Christ's crucifixion and glorification were virtually synonymous.

Note the comprehensive nature of our Lord's statement, 'will draw *all* men ['everyone', GNB] to myself.' Some commentators have found support in this for universalism, the belief that all people will in the end be saved, regardless of their choices. Such a view seems to overlook the context in which our Lord made this observation. Only a few sentences earlier he had said, 'The man who loves his life will lose it, while the man who hates his life in this world will keep it for eternal life.'

Immediately preceding the verse noted above, he had declared, 'Now is the time for judgment on this world', and he continued now with, 'now the prince of this world will be driven out'. Since that has not yet happened the judgment on the world must be distinct from the judgment on Satan. Judgment on the world, then, relates to those who, by disbelief, have rejected Christ and served Satan's ends.

Wonderfully and gloriously, the history of the Church glistens with accounts of men and women whose lives, once sinful, were drawn by the uplifted Christ into a true relationship with God. This same history glows because of the countless 'ordinary' people who, in like manner, also responded.

LEARNING OBEDIENCE

JOHN 13:36–38 – 'Peter asked, "Lord, why can't I follow you now? I will lay down my life for you"' (v. 37, NIV).

In this brief reading we are made aware of Peter's brash self-confidence and we see how Jesus warned him of his frailty. We can understand how a person of Peter's disposition would want to be where the action was. The command to love and to remain where he was seemed a poor substitute for being with the Master. He obviously sensed that such following involved danger and possible death, and wanted to know why he could not go with Jesus immediately (v. 37).

In what appears to be almost a throw-away comment, C.K. Barrett observed, 'Knowledge and religious experience are more attractive than obedience.' Peter had to learn the meaning of obedience. He had fulfilled the basic requirement of discipleship by *following* Jesus from the beginning (1:42) and the ultimate consequence of that must include following him to death and glory.

Peter's intentions, sincere as they were, are shown to have been centred in himself, in his own sense of inadequacy, and this was to prove his undoing. It would only be when the frailness of that self-confidence was exposed that Peter would find a sure foundation for faith and obedience.

There is a sense in which Peter's experience is typical of all who would discover a sure basis for discipleship. Following Jesus has to be the way of obedience to his will for us.

DESTINATION AND ROUTE

JOHN 14:1–14 – 'You must not let yourselves be distressed –
you must hold on to your faith in God, and to your faith in
me' (v. 1, JBP).

A few months before he was murdered, Charles de Foucauld, who
for many years maintained a lonely Christian witness among the
Muslims of North Africa, wrote, 'How good God is to hide from
us the future. What a torture life would be if this were known. And
how good of him, too, to show us so clearly his future in Heaven
which will follow these earthly trials.'

To disciples who were understandably distressed by their Master's
words about his 'going away', Jesus pointed to the ultimate goal
of the Christian life. There are times when nothing less will serve
to strengthen us. Nor need we be disturbed by the scoffer's jeer
about 'pie in the sky'. To limit one's perspective to this life alone
is inevitably to become confused by its apparent meaninglessness.
Only 'the eternal dimension' makes sense of the suffering inherent
in our present life.

The Christian, however, is not unhealthily obsessed with Heaven.
For this life he knows he needs guidance, direction and strength.
The truth of Christ's claim – 'I am the way and the truth and the
life' – can be proved only in experience. We begin, H.H. Farmer
said, with 'the soul's surmise' that these words are trustworthy.
Then, just as it is necessary to treat a man as a friend if we sense
he is capable of friendship, so we must commit ourselves to Christ's
way of life. As a result, what began as 'the soul's surmise' becomes
the soul's deepest conviction.

NO MERE COMPENSATION

JOHN 14:15–21 – 'And I will ask the Father, and he will give you another Counsellor to be with you for ever . . . I will not leave you as orphans, I will come to you' (vv. 16,18, NIV).

The Holy Spirit is both other than Christ and also the way Christ's presence is manifested following his ascension. This is the inescapable paradox of this passage where Jesus speaks of asking the Father to send 'another to be your Advocate', but also asserts, 'I am coming back to you.'

This means that we who never companioned with Christ in the flesh are by no means spiritually 'underprivileged'. We understand the feelings of the children's hymn writer:

I wish that his hands had been placed on my head,
That his arm had been thrown around me,
And that I might have seen his kind look when he said,
'Let the little ones come unto me'.

But by his Spirit Christ is as truly present with us today. The Holy Spirit, J.E. Fison wrote, 'is no mere compensation for what we have not got, and need, whether that be happiness or a clear conscience or friendship with the Lord Jesus Christ himself. He does not make up for the absence of Christ: he is the way to the presence of Christ.'

The experience of Christ's presence will come to different people in different ways. Simone Weil, the French mystic who died at the age of thirty-four, claimed that during prayer, 'Christ is present with me in person, but his presence is infinitely more real, more moving, more clear than on that first occasion when he took possession of me.' Yet most of us, for most of the time, lay hold of Christ's presence by faith rather than by feeling. And this is by no means to be regarded as a spiritual second-best.

COUNSELLOR, TEACHER, GUIDE

JOHN 14:25–31 – 'The Counsellor, the Holy Spirit, whom the
Father will send in my name, will teach you all things and will
remind you of everything I have said to you' (v. 26, NIV).

The above verse contains the first development of the teaching of
Jesus on the person and work of the Holy Spirit. The Counsellor
has already been referred to as 'the Spirit of truth' (v. 17); he is
now named 'the Holy Spirit'. He is sent by the Father in the name
of Jesus; that is – he will act with the authority of Jesus, in his
place, and in relation to all that Christ revealed in his teaching
and presence.

The first explicit statements of the Holy Spirit describe him as
teacher and *prompter*. Again, these are ideas which are more fully
developed in later chapters in John's Gospel. Here, in this present
statement, it is clear that, as *teacher*, he will reveal all that his
disciples will need to know for their life and service. As *prompter*
he will enable them to recall what Jesus had said and taught – and
to understand it.

Here we have the first picture of the Holy Spirit as the Church's
enabler – fitting Christ's followers for their mission in the first
century. But he also fulfils that same role for every generation
of follower since Pentecost. And this is good news for today and
tomorrow . . . and tomorrow . . . and tomorrow. We should continue
to pray for the guidance and instruction of the Holy Spirit – for us
– today!

UNION WITH CHRIST

JOHN 15:1–8 – 'I am the vine; you are the branches. If a man remains in me and I in him, he will bear much fruit; apart from me you can do nothing' (v. 5, NIV).

In the Old Testament the vine and vineyard are used as symbols of God's chosen people, Israel. This can be seen in such passages as Psalm 80:1–16; Isaiah 5:1–7; and Jeremiah 2:21. The same symbolism is carried through into several parables of the first three Gospels: Matthew 20:1–16; 21:28–32; Mark 12:1–9; and Luke 13:6–9.

If these references are compared with the reading above, from John's Gospel, it will be noticed that one obvious change has taken place. The vine no longer refers to Israel but to Jesus himself. 'I am the vine', he declares (v. 5, see also v. 1). Other changes have also taken place. Instead of a parable, these verses have become an allegory based upon the care and nurture of the vines. The purpose of an allegory is to provide a number of facets of truth, and this makes the present passage rich in meaning for us today.

Israel had failed through lack of faithfulness to God, and to the covenant they had made with him. By contrast, not only by reason of his birth and his divine sonship, but also through his obedience, Jesus was the true vine.

Only insofar as Christians live in union with Christ do they experience the vitality which marks them out as the new people of God. That relationship produces fruitfulness (vv. 4,5), conformity to Christ's nature, communion in prayer, and obedience in love (v. 7).

There are also serious warnings for those who would try to 'go it alone' (vv. 2a,4b,6). 'Apart from me you can do nothing' is perhaps the most powerful warning of all.

28

PROGRESSIVE UNDERSTANDING

JOHN 16:1–15 – ' "I have much more to say to you, more than you can now bear" ' (v. 12, NIV).

Jesus promised that the Holy Spirit would lead his disciples into understanding which was quite beyond them at present; for our capacity determines our grasp of God's revelation. Let us relate this fact to the way we teach our children (and others), and our own spiritual quest.

We must ensure, as far as possible, that the religious teaching we give to children never needs to be unlearned. True, it will later need expansion, but it should never need expulsion. For the disciples, there was no going back upon the truth given them by Jesus – only a subsequent deepening and widening of that truth. Careless and makeshift teaching of the young cannot be excused on the grounds that later years give opportunity for correction.

For ourselves we must recognise that the Spirit will carry us forward into new understanding only as we patiently and watchfully heed his movements in our hearts. Reminding his readers that the Spirit is frequently likened to the wind, a leader writer in *The Friend* wrote: 'A man who takes up dinghy sailing does not know immediately where the wind is coming from . . . winds do not blow steadily; they freshen and die away and then come in from a new quarter . . . he has to haul his sheet a little when the wind moves aft, and sometimes change direction when faced with a calm patch.'

So must the believer watch for the movements of the Spirit among his fellows and in his own heart if he would be carried forward progressively into truth.

PRIESTLY INTERCESSION

JOHN 17:1–10 – 'Jesus . . . looked towards heaven and prayed: "Father, the time has come"' (v. 1, NIV).

The one long continuous prayer of Jesus recorded in the Gospels is found in this chapter. It is called the 'high priestly' prayer because in it Jesus intercedes for his followers, and consecrates himself to the sacrifice of the Cross.

Each verse of this prayer provides rich material for meditation. Let us concentrate, however, on the fact of Christ's intercession. For while we have no other lengthy record of this ministry, we know that Jesus often prayed for his disciples (Luke 22:32), and the New Testament asserts that he continues to intercede for us in Heaven (Hebrews 7:25). As an underground stream gushes out of the rock, to delight the eye before being lost to sight farther on, so the intercessory ministry of Jesus comes to the surface in this wonderful chapter.

This will mean little to us if we hold the widely accepted, but quite erroneous, view that intercession is telling God what he already knows, or asking God for favours he is reluctant to bestow. Intercession is one way in which divine energies are released into the world, one method, which we by no means fully understand, by which man co-operates with God.

That Christ intercedes for us is a thought of infinite encouragement: that our own intercessions are linked with his can keep us faithful in the place of prayer.

Part 2

MIGHTY MEN OF ISRAEL

The Bible is filled with stories of people – all kinds of people: saints and villains, high born and low born, warriors and shepherds, old and young . . . When God wanted to reveal some great and wonderful truth to the world he did so through *people*. In the Old Testament especially he revealed himself and his purposes through the Hebrews, a people chosen by him as the vehicle of the revelation of his love to the whole world. Sadly, these chosen ones often forgot that aspect of their calling and there developed among them a strong sense of national exclusiveness, that they were the *only* people of God. The Bible has a great deal to say about that.

The people of the Bible were real flesh and blood people like us. We, of course, live in a very different world from that of the Bible, but we are not greatly different *inwardly* from those whose stories are told in the Scriptures. Human hopes and fears, motives and longings are pretty much the same as they always were. People are still people.

This section focuses on some of the 'mighty men' (as we may call them) of the Old Testament, by which is meant those who *did* things, the activists. There is another class of people, prominent and important in the Old Testament, who were 'mighty' too, but in a different way. Their greatness lay in their understanding of the mind and purposes of God, and their readiness, often at great personal cost, to convey their messages to the people. They are the so-called 'writing' prophets and we shall be looking at some of these later in this book.

Here, though, we look at men like Moses, Samson, Joshua and David and see what they have to tell us. It has to be said, however, that the division of the Bible people into 'activists' and 'thinkers' cannot be exact. Moses, David and others of them were thinkers

31

as well as men of action; and some of the prophets were 'doers'. But in a broad sense, the people featured in this section were men who *did* things.

But these 'activists', no less than the prophets, have a great deal to say to us. Sometimes their activities convey warnings; often they bring positive and encouraging messages just by what they did. But they always inform; they tell us important things about God. Our study of some of them, and their deeds, should be a rewarding exercise.

THE DIVINE COMMAND

GENESIS 12:1–5 – ' "Leave your country, your people, and
your father's household" ' (v. 1, NIV).

God called Abraham to leave everything – all that was familiar,
all that had supported him, all that had provided security and
protection. He called him and his wife to step out into the unknown,
and he assured them of his blessing.

So God comes to people; not necessarily calling them to move
from one country to another, but calling them to place their utter
trust in him and to do as he directs. His demands are absolute; it
is only God who can rightfully ask so much, and only he who can
be trusted with so much.

On the thirtieth anniversary of his marriage to Catherine, William
Booth recalled the early days of their life together. 'On two separate
occasions since our married life,' he said, 'and once before we had
married, I had literally gone out, for conscience' sake, into the
darkness as far as earthly support has been concerned, leaving
all the friends that we had made. When these steps have been
premeditated, which have had such bearing upon home and earthly
comforts, my beloved wife stood by me and said, "William, never
you consider me. I can trust God and go out with him . . . go out
and do your duty!" '

God's demands come to us in different ways, for God has different
purposes for each of us to accomplish. But for everyone the nature
of his demand is the same: it is to leave all else – and trust *him*.

OFFERED TO GOD

GENESIS 22:1–18 – 'You have not withheld from me your son, your only son' (v. 12, NEB).

When we have shared with Abraham something of his longing for a son and his great rejoicing when at last Isaac was born, we can enter more fully into the events connected with his offering Isaac as a sacrifice to God. Abraham had waited almost a lifetime for this son, and God had finally fulfilled his promise to him. Once Abraham had thought his line might be through another young boy, but it had become evident that was not to be. Ishmael and his mother had been sent away. Only Isaac was left. And now *he* had to be sacrificed.

What was it like on Mount Moriah? The fifteenth-century wood-carver Ghiberti created a smooth, classical picture of the angel gliding down from heaven to prevent the sacrifice. On the other hand Ghiberti's contemporary Brunelleschi saw Moriah as the scene of a violent struggle. We must use our imagination and insight. When the realisation dawned upon Abraham that his *willingness* to sacrifice Isaac was enough, did he snatch his son from the woodpile, hug him close, and weep tears of joy over him?

From that point on, Abraham's relationship with Isaac must have taken on a new depth of meaning. Abraham had taken his only son – and given him to God. Isaac, of course, remained his son, but now in a peculiar way he was God's and he always would be. The strange thing that Abraham discovered was because Isaac was God's, he was now more truly his own.

UNPROMISING START

GENESIS 25:19–21,24–28 – 'Isaac, who had a taste for wild game, loved Esau, but Rebekah loved Jacob' (v. 28, NIV).

This is the point in the Genesis narrative when the spotlight falls upon Jacob, whose twelve sons were to become the fathers of the twelve tribes of Israel. With his twin brother Esau he was born in answer to his father's intercessions.

'All happy families are alike, but an unhappy family is unhappy after its own fashion.' So wrote Leo Tolstoy at the beginning of his book *Anna Karenina*, and it would seem that the number of family patterns are legion. Certainly, Jacob had an unpromising beginning. He became a mother's boy, perhaps just because his father so obviously preferred Esau. We now know how important it is for the growing child to identify with the parent of the same sex. Failure to do so frequently results in lifelong uncertainty and lack of confidence. This has to be compensated for by bluff or subtlety. The family situation described in this reading is exactly the one most likely to produce the grasping, scheming Jacob later encountered in the narrative.

What a mercy God's choice does not fall only on those with faultless upbringing, or those blessed with attractive personality! Jacob had neither, but he became 'a prince with God'.

CAN'T WAIT

GENESIS 25:29–34 – 'Esau despised his birthright' (v. 34, NIV).

Neither Jacob nor Esau plays an admirable role in this story. Jacob is the typical opportunist, ready to exploit his brother's weakness for his own advantage. Esau reveals a childish need to grasp immediate satisfaction no matter what the long-term consequences. The Bible writer particularly notes Esau's scornful disregard for his birthright, which had religious as well as material significance. 'If he was defrauded, he was defrauded of that which he was incapable of appreciating.'

Esau lived only for the present moment. Now we certainly need to live fully and completely *in* the present moment. All too often we forfeit the enjoyment of beauty – sunlight setting a puddle on fire, the cascade of children's laughter – because we are imprisoned in yesterday's disappointments. Frequently we miss our chance to help because we are engrossed in tomorrow's projects. We need to value and learn fully how to savour each moment as it is given to us.

Yet this is not the same as living *only* for the present. To do this is to make a shipwreck of life and is a denial of every religious insight. The writer to the Hebrews held up Esau as a stern warning: he also told his readers to fix their eyes on Jesus who, 'for the sake of the joy that lay before him, endured the Cross' (12:2, NEB).

THE PERILS OF SUCCESS

GENESIS 37:3–11 – 'Now Israel loved Joseph more than any other of his children' (v. 3, RSV).

A study of the life of Jacob (here named Israel) and Joseph's brothers is a rewarding exercise, but here, now, we look at Joseph himself. There is no doubt as to his potential greatness – later events proved it – but it was nearly crushed in his early years. His father's favouritism could so easily have ruined his character, and this would have been more serious than the physical destruction to which his brother's envy almost led.

But Joseph survived, developed morally and prospered. Yet the deplorable characteristics he displayed in his youth explain, if they do not justify, his brothers' attitude to him. It is not difficult to imagine the seventeen-year-old lad showing off his coat, sign of his father's special favour, and he doubtless derived satisfaction in recounting his dreams in which his family made obeisance to him. Joseph had to learn that the ambition to be successful must not get out of hand. Can any of us learn other than the hard way?

Saintly missionary Temple Gairdner, of Cairo, wrote: 'I have found ambition dreadfully difficult to cope with,' and Harry Emerson Fosdick tells, in his autobiography, how his early successes in college did him more harm than good. Prize after prize went Fosdick's way and he commented, 'Fewer winnings and more defeats would have been salutary. I may have been heading for the ministry, but I was not distinguished for meekness.'

Though it is not always easy to see, it is profoundly true that those 'of a gentle spirit' do inherit the earth. Saints attain that place of spiritual maturity. It is the goal we lesser people must keep in view.

GOD'S HAND IN LIFE'S ILLS

GENESIS 45:1–15 – 'It was God who sent me ahead of you to save men's lives' (v. 5, NEB).

The climax of the great story of Joseph is reached as he looks into the faces of his incredulous brothers saying, 'I am Joseph.' They were obviously not prepared for his magnanimity as he went on: 'Do not be distressed . . . God sent me ahead of you to save men's lives.' These generous words show the nobility of the man. If there were space we could pause here to note our Christian duty to return love for hate and to be generous towards those we find it hard to like. That is an important lesson we can learn from this incident.

But the significance of this passage goes even deeper than that. Joseph's words mean that though God had not willed the brothers' cruelty and deceit, he was not defeated by them. He can bring victory out of the apparent disasters of life.

Too many of us are still living in the spirit of the Old Testament where disasters were thought to be signs of God's displeasure and his blessing and approval were proved by material prosperity. We need to learn that this is not God's way. He does not 'wrap us up in cotton wool' and thus keep us babes all our lives. We have to face inconvenience, ills and tragedies. Such encourage us to grow towards maturity and help us to become the kind of people God wants us to be.

GOD WORKS THROUGH PEOPLE

EXODUS 2:1–10 – 'So the woman took the baby and nursed him. When the child grew older, she took him to Pharaoh's daughter and he became her son. She named him Moses' (vv. 9,10, NIV).

The story of Moses is really the story of God's greatness, providence and deeds. He, and not the man, is the central figure in the chapter of Hebrew history that begins here in this passage of Scripture. The education of Moses, his training for leadership under the best Egyptian tutors and all that this meant for his future work as leader of God's people, stemmed, humanly speaking, from Pharaoh's plan to destroy all the male children born to the Hebrew slaves, because he now saw those people as a threat to his nation's security. But it was God who, working through the intentions of the Egyptian ruler, utilised them for the furtherance of his own divine purposes.

Here is an important truth. God works in history through people, ordinary people like Moses' mother, with her longing to save her son from death; people of outstanding ability like Moses himself (for so he proved to be) and even – most staggering of all – people like Pharaoh who had ideas that ran counter to God's own.

There are two important applications of this truth. In the first place it cuts us down to size when we grow proud of what we imagine to be our own generous and competent contribution to the cause of God's kingdom. It is what *he* does that counts; we are only people, with all the weaknesses of our humanity. Yet – and this is the second application of the truth – despite our frailties God chooses to develop his purpose through us. What an astonishing, humbling yet exhilarating thought!

HOW PHARAOH HURT HIMSELF

EXODUS 5:1–14 – ' "Who is the Lord", asked Pharaoh, "that I should obey him and let Israel go?" ' (v. 2, NEB).

Forty years after he had exchanged the splendours of the Egyptian court for the hazards and privations of the desert, Moses returned. Armed with nothing more than a shepherd's rod, and accompanied only by his brother, he re-entered the magnificent palace of Pharaoh. (A different Pharaoh from forty years before, so the danger from which Moses had fled was now past.) His request that the Hebrew people be given a temporary release to exercise a religious duty seemed reasonable enough, though not, evidently, to an unreasonable man as Pharaoh proved himself to be. He saw Moses' request as a pretext for his people to have a holiday, and as evidence that they were not fully occupied, so he not only refused the request but made it an excuse to lay further burdens on the already overtaxed people.

This was a grave set-back for Moses, for he saw his genuine concern for his people working out to their sorrow, always a hard thing to bear. Was he also tempted to see this as confirmation of his earlier fears that the task was too hard for him?

Yet, though Pharaoh's action brought sorrow to Moses and his people, it hurt Pharaoh himself even more. He cannot be blamed for his ignorance concerning the God of the Hebrews, of course, but he stands condemned for his disregard for the sufferings of the people Moses represented. Utter insensitivity to the claims of love might be expected in a pagan potentate, but it always dehumanises and therefore impoverishes. Certainly, we must not forget that the depth of our relationship with God is measured by our awareness of the needs of others.

THE COVENANT RATIFIED

EXODUS 24:1–18 – 'He took the book of the covenant and read it aloud for all the people to hear. They said, "We will obey, and do all that the Lord has said"' (vv. 7,8, NEB).

On Sinai the Children of Israel received the Ten Commandments (20:1–17) and also a code of laws regulating aspects of their worship and their social and domestic life. Called the Book of the Covenant, this code is set out in chapters 20:18 to 23:33. There follows in the above passage the account of the ratification of the covenant.

It was a great moment in Israel's history when the people promised to keep all the words of their God. On one side stood Yahweh, represented by the altar Moses built; on the other side stood the people. An animal was killed and the blood sprinkled on the two contracting parties, who were then united by the 'life' (the shed blood) of the sacrificial victim.

It was a richly symbolic ceremony. Inadequate in itself (as Jeremiah was later to show – Jeremiah 31:32–34) it nevertheless points to the New Covenant inaugurated and sealed by Jesus Christ. In him the atonement is made between God and people; in him God has pledged himself to mankind for ever. This is the theme and the heart of the biblical revelation. From Noah, through Abraham and Moses, the concept of the covenant persists until we see it in its highest and ultimate form in the New Testament.

Though the Old Testament can only partially reveal God's grace, and though, despite the fuller revelation in Jesus, our own comprehension is limited by our poor vision, the marvellous fact is that God has always loved people – and loves them still. In view of this, the pessimism and despair of which we are frequently guilty are quite unnecessary.

THE BEST OF WORDS OF LIFE

FALSE IMAGES – METAL AND MENTAL

EXODUS 31:18–32:6 – 'He . . . cast the metal in a mould, and made it into the image of a bull-calf' (v. 4, NEB).

After the ratification of the covenant Moses went up the mountain and stayed there for forty days and nights (24:18). This reading continues from there. The prolonged absence of their leader, however, gave rise to impatience and doubts in the Israelites, and led to the making of the famous (or notorious) golden calf. Their intention was not to displace Yahweh with another god (which the first commandment strictly forbade) but to provide a representation of him, something they could *see* – but this was in violation of the second commandment. They intended to worship Yahweh *through* the image. But the danger with such an image was that it might so easily cut down God to the size of the object by which he was being represented.

It is a danger to which we, with our *mental* images, are as open as were the Israelites with their *metal* images. We give God names like Father, King, Shepherd because, being human, we need such images. But no image can truly represent him; he must always be bigger and more wonderful than the best of them.

There are some Christians who appear to have ideas about God which bear little resemblance to the truth. They credit him with attitudes and actions not easily found in human beings. 'It is God's will,' they declare piously when, say, a little child is killed on the road or a young man dies of a cruel disease, instead of acknowledging the mystery in such events, while holding to the Bible's affirmation that, despite all that might appear to deny it, *God is love*.

Any image of God that does not conform to the mind of Christ must be firmly rejected for, as the New Testament reveals, *God is like Jesus*.

42

THE COST OF INTERCESSION

EXODUS 32:30–35 – 'So Moses went back to the Lord and said, "Oh, what a great sin these people have committed! . . . But now please forgive their sin – but if not, then blot me out of the book you have written"' (vv. 31,32, NIV).

On the mountain Moses prays that God might not destroy his people and fashion another out of himself. Then he comes down from the mountain, sees the golden calf, and in his anger breaks the tablets of stone on which the commandments are engraved. He sternly upbraids Aaron and those with him for what they had done. All this is recorded in the first verses of this chapter, and it would be an advantage to read the account. Then, picking up the story in the above reading, we see that Moses went to God in prayer to make further intercession on behalf of his people.

In this second prayer the nobility of Moses is again revealed as he pleads for the people, asking that if they cannot be forgiven, he be allowed to share the punishment with them. Now, while we are clearly shown here that it is not God's wish that a man trade his own salvation for the salvation of another – notice that God refused Moses' offer – the incident does emphasise for us the costly nature of intercession.

Too many of our prayers for others can so easily be a mere mouthing of words. To remember others' needs before God is important and valuable, of course, but what does that lead to in terms of personal sacrifice? Are our prayers for a distressed friend, for instance, followed by a visit and a sympathetic – though never condescending – offer of practical help? Do our prayers for the stricken in another land prompt us to write our cheque for the fund being launched on their behalf?

In one way or another intercession is costly, for to love deeply will not only send us to our knees, it will also constrain us to *do something*.

THE WHOLENESS OF LIFE

JOSHUA 1:1–9 – '"Do not let this Book of the Law depart from your mouth; meditate on it day and night, so that you may be careful to do everything written in it"' (v. 8, NIV).

The prime requirement that was laid upon Joshua was that he should observe diligently the law of the Lord, and he was assured that he would then prosper in all he did. Now the extent to which this was proved in practice we may observe as we read his story, but perhaps the writer's ideas were a little too neat. There *is* a correspondence between a man's faith in God and his subsequent living, but the saints have not always prospered in earthly terms.

Yet Joshua does remind us that religion is an integral part of life. For the Israelites religion was not apart from the everyday; life was a whole and a man's relationship with God had a direct bearing on his daily existence. Today, of course, society has changed greatly from those days, and people generally are not as conscious of God in the field of their experience.

Yet this is all the more reason for the believer to realise that religion is not something on top of, or extra to, life. True religion, proclaims the Christian, is the heart of all life. Reading the story of Joshua will help us to see just what this means for us.

> *So shall no part of day or night*
> *From sacredness be free;*
> *But all my life, in every step,*
> *Be fellowship with thee.*
> *Horatius Bonar*

SACRIFICIAL IDENTIFICATION

JOSHUA 1:10–18 – 'You must help them, until the Lord grants them security like you' (vv. 14,15, NEB).

The book of Joshua presents the conquest of Canaan as being a national affair. Some tribes had already been allotted land east of the Jordan, but for the invasion their fighting men had to join the other tribes – indeed, to go at their head – until all the land had been subdued. They would rest when all could rest.

A similar identification with the needs of others was seen in the life of John White, a Methodist missionary among the Mashona people of what was then Southern Rhodesia. At a time when the Mashona were suffering cruelly during fighting in the area, he chose to stay with them and risked his life to give them support and some leadership. He wrote to a friend: 'What a pleasure it would be to come home!' But he felt that God had put him in the front of the strife and there he stayed.

'In the world at large', said Barbara Ward in 1968, 'we are still "tribalists". The child that starves in distant Bihar is not our child. The millions without land and bread in Latin America lie beyond the limits of our imagination . . . For us, the humanity for which we feel a full moral obligation runs up to the frontier.'

Have we progressed since then? We must cease being 'tribalists', cease drawing the boundaries of our own compassion at our own 'frontier' – whatever that frontier might be. As our needs have been supplied, we must learn how to identify sacrificially with the needs of others.

A KEY VIRTUE

JUDGES 6:11–16 – ' "But Lord," Gideon asked, "how can
I save Israel? My clan is the weakest in Manasseh, and I am
the least in my family" ' (v. 15, NIV).

Midian was a nomadic people and made no attempt at permanent
conquest. They waited while surrounding tribes and nations worked
at sowing and cultivation, then raided a chosen territory in time
to reap the harvest. During their temporary occupation they were
cruelly oppressive. It was owing to this that Gideon was threshing
wheat – usually done in an exposed place where the wind helped
to blow away the chaff – in a winepress.

Although God's messenger addressed Gideon as a 'mighty
warrior' (v. 12), Gideon's self-assessment was much less exalted.
Throughout the Bible the men God chooses usually receive their
vocation with the utmost surprise. They are a highly varied
company: soldiers, politicians, shepherds, priests and prophets.
One qualification they commonly possess is humility. They endorse
the hymn writer's claim:

All the fitness he requireth
Is to feel your need of him.

It is easy to see why humility, which is not self-disparagement but
realistic self-assessment, is a key virtue, once we grasp the truth
that pride is the root sin. Yet this we are most loath to do, for
we cling tenaciously to anything that elevates us a little above our
fellows!

John Baillie wrote: 'Some indeed have preferred to say that the
essence of all sin is selfishness, while others, thinking of how difficult
they find it to keep the body under . . . have said that it is rather
sensuality . . . But it is much easier to see how selfishness and
sensuality have their root in pride than to see how pride has its
roots in them.'

A SPRING OF COMFORT

JUDGES 15:1–20 – 'Then God opened up the hollow place in Lehi, and water came out of it. When Samson drank, his strength returned and he revived' (v. 19, NIV).

Samson was the scourge of the Philistines – as this chapter shows – and was naturally a hero to his fellow-Israelites. From our religious point of view, his earthiness, lack of spiritual vision and his ungodliness make it difficult for us to recognise him as God's man for the hour. If, however, we accept the perspective of the writer of the book of Judges, that he was born to 'begin the deliverance of Israel from the hands of the Philistines' (13:5), we may understand him better. Even so, when we read of him being a Nazarite and empowered by the Spirit of the Lord, our expectations far exceed his performance.

Not unreasonably, Samson found that the killing of one thousand men, using only the jaw-bone of a donkey, was thirsty work and, in the absence of a supply of water, he cried out to God for help. Wisely, he ascribed to God his victory over the Philistines, indicating that without water he would die, and his body be left a trophy for the Philistines (v. 18). Immediately, out of a hollow in the ground, a spring of water began to flow. God had not failed his thirsty and probably discouraged champion.

Matthew Henry described this miracle flow of life-reviving water as a 'spring of comfort'. It is a happy description that fits our own experiences. Have we not been in extreme need at some time or other and God, in his delightful way, has provided a word of assurance, an act of kindness, or a special insight which has been, for us, a spring of comfort?

AN UNIMAGINED LOSS

JUDGES 16:18–22 – 'He did not know that the Lord had left him' (v. 20, NIV).

These are among the saddest words in the Bible. Having lived a privileged life, sheltered from his enemies by God, basking in the adulation of his peers, Samson probably believed that he could continue to indulge his lower nature indefinitely. But God's tolerance level had obviously been reached. He would no longer support a man who disregarded his role in Israel and ignored the laws so wisely given.

After he had fallen asleep with his head cradled in Delilah's lap, Samson had his head shaved by her and, because his strength was related to his Nazarite vow with its condition of uncut hair (Numbers 6:5), his strength ebbed away and he became as vulnerable as other men. When Delilah woke him with the cry, 'Samson, the Philistines are upon you!' he was unable to respond as before because the Lord had left him.

King Saul was another who commenced his public life with substantial advantages, but allowed his life to get out of control, and it was written of him: 'Now the Spirit of the Lord had departed from Saul.' In his case the Spirit of the Lord was replaced by an evil spirit, but the latter must have been in the ascendancy for some time.

Have we not been witnesses of this sad experience? Are there not people we have known whose value to us has been considerable, whom we have admired, treating them as examples to follow, only for them to be overtaken in a sin and lost to us? On subsequent reflection we have probably been able to identify an occasion when, had we been more sensitive at the time, we would have known the power had gone from them. The Spirit of the Lord was no longer their strength and guide. The prayer of all of us should be: 'Come give us still thy powerful aid, And urge us on and keep us thine . . .' (Cecil Frances Alexander).

PICTURE OF FAMILY LIFE

1 SAMUEL 1:1–8 – 'Her husband Elkanah would ask her, "Hannah, why are you crying? Why won't you eat? Why are you always so sad? Don't I mean more to you than ten sons?"' (v. 8, GNB).

Samuel's childhood may seem irrelevant to the course of Jewish history, but it has great relevance to our understanding of family life. Elkanah's brash insensitivity to Hannah's feelings – her psychological need to bear children emphasised by the social stigma attached to childlessness – is painfully true to life.

Hannah had other troubles. There was another woman in her husband's life – his number two wife, Peninnah, who, to make matters worse, had children and lost no opportunity to attack Hannah at the very point where she should have shown sympathy. Yet perhaps Peninnah's spite erupted from the fact that although she had almost everything a woman could want, she did not have Hannah's position as number one wife and her place in Elkanah's affections.

But it was Elkanah's tactlessness that was 'the unkindest cut of all'. First, he instituted a 'fair shares for all' policy, dividing 'the housekeeping money' into equal shares, one for each member of the family – one for Hannah, and the rest for Peninnah and her children. Fair perhaps, but it rubbed salt in the wound. Then there was Elkanah's 'good-humoured' attitude to the problem. He made a joke of it all, but was really a little more than half in earnest when he said to her, 'You've got me! What more do you want?'

We should ask the Lord to bless all women who cannot have children, and to curb those who act spitefully when sympathy is called for and those who regard the troubles of others as a joke.

FIRST-HAND RELIGION

1 SAMUEL 3:1–9 – 'Then Eli realised that it was the Lord who was calling the boy, so he said to him, "Go back to bed; and if he calls again, say, 'Speak, Lord, your servant is listening'"' (vv. 8,9, GNB).

Samuel's prompt response to what he thought was the voice of Eli suggests that he would have been even more ready to respond to God's voice. The difficulty was that he had no experience, or expectation, of hearing it. His religion had been a matter of learning from elders and fulfilling religious duties.

This is the pattern of much childhood piety, but sooner or later there must come a challenge to personal knowledge of, and response to, God. Samuel's second-hand religion was dangerous because there was no climate of expectation in the priesthood or the nation to cause him to have any dissatisfaction with it. He had had no personal revelation (v. 8), but neither had anybody else (v. 1). Even Eli was very slow to recognise the symptoms of direct revelation.

Of Catherine Booth it is said that, 'It was an illness at the age of fourteen which ensured that she formulated her own beliefs. For twelve months she lay on her back in an attempt to rectify a spinal defect; during that time she read the Bible and books relating to the Christian faith. The knowledge and conviction which came to her then were to shape her future.'

A question: does our religion consist merely of second-hand truths and habitual duties? And a prayer: 'O Jesus, be thyself to me a living, bright reality.'

ON BEING OURSELVES

1 SAMUEL 17:19–39 – 'Then Saul dressed David in his own tunic. He put a coat of armour on him . . . "I cannot go in these," [David] said to Saul, "because I am not used to them." So he took them off' (vv. 38,39, NIV).

David found that Saul's armour did not fit him and that he could not therefore copy Saul's method of fighting. The shepherd boy was different from the king and must make his contribution to the defeat of the Philistines in his own way. It was because David acted as himself and not as another that the giant was slain.

There are some people who lament the fact that they are not like so-and-so; they do not possess *her* presence, or *his* talents. Such an attitude has one of two effects. It either leads people to despair at their own supposed inferiority, or it prompts them to a foolish aping of others. Both results are likely to lead to a warping of the personality. Hero worship in childhood and youth is natural and healthy enough, but few things are sadder than to see grown men or women pathetically striving to pattern their lives and conduct on another. The message for such people is: 'Recognise you are a person in your own right!' and even, 'Assert yourself!' There is a place for renunciation in Christian life, but only after a man has found himself has he anything to renounce.

God wants us to be ourselves. He made us different from every other being; we are each unique and unrepeatable because he wants us that way. Let us recognise the truth, which is both humbling and exhilarating, that God accepts us and is able to use us not despite but because of what we are!

HOW TO SLAY OUR GIANTS

1 SAMUEL 17:40–58 – 'The Lord who delivered me from the paw of the lion and the paw of the bear will deliver me from the hand of this Philistine' (v. 37, NIV).

According to 2 Samuel 21:19 Goliath's destruction was the work of one Elhanan, though somehow David seems to have received the credit for it! But even if it was the obscure Elhanan who killed Goliath there can be little doubt that David also slew a giant and his name is not of the first importance – only that David did it. In the strength of that exploit alone David may be accounted a hero, for giant-killers are heroes, as every child in the nursery knows!

Indeed, giant-killing may be said to be a theme of life. Dwarfed by the problems of a dangerous world, mocked by forces that threaten to overwhelm us, we put a great deal of energy into slaying the monsters that block the path to our inner peace. Yet are we wise to do so? Is success assured by our own feverish activity?

As we look beyond the details of this well-known story to the spiritual truths it symbolises, we learn the source of victory in living. This comes not by arrogance, pride and the trust in human resources we see in the Philistine, but in the calm confidence in the living God shown in the youthful David.

The redemptive power of love is revealed supremely in Jesus, and in this may be found our sure and complete victory over the weaknesses and sins that so easily beset us.

FAULTY HUMAN RELATIONSHIPS

1 SAMUEL 20:24–34 – 'Saul hurled his spear at him to kill him. Then Jonathan knew that his father intended to kill David' (v. 33, NIV).

'The story of the hostility between Saul and David,' observed John Mauchline in his book, *God's People Israel*, 'illustrates nothing so much as the truth that a little spark may kindle a great fire. In healing quarrels as in mending garments a stitch in time saves nine. That stitch was never effectively applied in the quarrel between Saul and David; pride may have been the cause of the failure; and the end was doubtless what neither desired; but there comes a time in strained relationships when to give in seems inexcusable weakness; after that no healing is possible and the end is bitter.'

Tragically enough, the principle may be seen operating in our own everyday relationships. How many bitter quarrels – between friends, father and child, husband and wife – begin with minor disagreements which, because of stubborn pride, grow out of all proportion to their origin so that eventually relationships are severely ruptured and in some cases irrevocably broken? Willingness to see the other's point of view; readiness to forgive and be forgiven; grace to 'pocket one's pride' – these are essential to enduring relationships. In other words we need to *work at* our friendships, our marriage and other relationships if we want them to deepen.

But in addition we need at all times to seek divine grace. We may successfully sustain and deepen our human relationships in the context of the relationship 'par excellence' – with God himself.

CHOOSING BETWEEN TWO RIGHTS

2 SAMUEL 9:1–13 – 'David asked, "Is there anyone still left of the house of Saul to whom I can show kindness for Jonathan's sake?"' (v. 1, NIV).

According to the thinking of his day, David would have been exercising political wisdom in disposing of the surviving members of Saul's family. But he had made a solemn covenant to preserve them, and so found that an obligation to the state conflicted with his obligation to the dead king.

Life involves us all in the complex business of making choices. If it were always a matter of choosing between obvious wrong and unambiguous right it would be an easy matter. But there are peculiar difficulties in conflicting *obligations*, the choice between two *rights*.

Situations of this kind may arise in family relationships: a man's obligation to his church or firm, perhaps, conflicts with his obligation to family and home. There is no easy solution; no sure formula to success. David chose to give priority to the covenant he made with Jonathan, though in doing so he was probably putting the peace and security of the state at risk. In making his agonising decision he had to use his reason, but because of what we know of him it cannot be doubted that he trusted God to guide him. Reason and trust are not in opposition; Christians use both.

We may not expect to make unerring judgments on every problem that arises, nor to be always free from perplexity. But with a firm trust in God we shall not utterly fail.

THE SIN OF APATHY

2 SAMUEL 15:1–15 – 'Absalom . . . stole the hearts of the men of Israel' (v. 6, NIV).

Absalom's rebellion had its roots in David's apathy and neglect. In the first place, David ought to have taken firm action against Amnon, his son, for the shameful outrage he perpetrated against Tamar, his half-sister and Absalom's full sister (2 Samuel 13:1–15). It was this incident which provided Absalom with the excuse for taking the law into his own hands and which led to the rebellion against the crown, and his father.

But David turned a blind eye to the misdeeds of his greatly loved first-born, and lived to pay the price of his neglect. 'Take care that you do not sin against [your children's] souls,' wrote W. Pearson Halliday, 'in not being wise as the serpent in the ways of the world . . . The love which is blind is the love which brings a curse in its wake.' Most painfully David was to learn the truth of that.

It was David's neglect, also, which allowed Absalom to worm his way into the affections of the people by playing on their feeling of deprivation. The king seemed to prefer ease to duty and was failing to give his subjects redress for their complaints. He paid dearly for this further expression of his apathy, by losing their confidence.

We may apply this to the wider relationships of life, recalling the famous saying of Edmund Burke: 'All that is required for the triumph of evil is that good men do nothing.' The power of the silent witness of the good life to rebuke wrong must not be underestimated, but it should not be forgotten that, when it is time for positive (if costly) action, silence and apathy are sin.

THE CONFLICT GOES ON

1 KINGS 17:1–6 – 'Elijah the Tishbite . . . said to Ahab, "As the Lord, the God of Israel, lives, whom I serve, there will be neither rain nor dew in the next few years at my word"' (v. 1, NIV).

Elijah's appearance upon the stage of Israel's history was sudden and dramatic. We read nothing of his birth or parentage and, typical of this doughty fighter for God, the record opens with him challenging Ahab the king. By tolerating the idolatrous worship which his wife Jezebel had introduced into Israel, Ahab was jeopardising both the nation's religion and its ethical standards. Elijah became Ahab's fearless opponent, and succeeded in halting the nation's backsliding. What Israel owed to him can never be measured.

The conflict between good and evil is inseparable from human history, and in this battle neutrality is impossible. Sometimes the issues are less clear cut than they were in Elijah's day – it is then that the danger of complacency is greatest. We need the reminder of William James: 'If this life be not a real fight in which something is eternally gained for the universe by success, it is no better than a game of private theatricals from which one may withdraw at will. But it *feels* like a real fight – as if there were something really wild in the universe which we, with our idealities and faithfulnesses, are needed to redeem . . .'

In the conflict between good and evil we are strengthened to remember that evil is the intruder – only goodness is eternal and therefore undefeatable. The words of Nicholas Berdyaev provide us with a 'thought for the day': 'Christians are living in this sinful world and must bear its burden; they must not steal away from the battlefield.'

CONFRONTATION

1 KINGS 18:1–39 – 'Elijah replied . . . "Summon the people from all over Israel to meet me on Mount Carmel"' (vv. 18,19, NIV).

To strengthen the position of his country, King Omri made a 'diplomatic marriage' for his son Ahab. The bride was Jezebel, daughter of the King of Sidon. Israel's religion was already rotten with the nature cults of Canaan, and the new queen was not only a worshipper of the Tyrian god, she was an active missionary. The word 'baal' means master, husband, or local god. Now the ancient nature gods of Canaan were reinforced by the great Baal of Tyre.

Against the imperious queen and her vacillating husband stood the 'prophets of the Lord', and the rugged Elijah. He came from Gilead, east of the Jordan, that semi-desert country where the faith of Israel had been less contaminated – for, unlike the farmer, the nomad has no need to please the local godlings. Elijah confronts King Ahab and proposes a test (v. 19): Which God is able to end the drought? Rain-making was a speciality of the Baal of Tyre, and therefore Elijah was proposing to meet the opposition on its own ground.

The authors of the books of Kings were wise to highlight this contest, which is another turning point in the history of religion, for the baals were only natural forces personified, while Elijah believed in a living, personal Creator. As long as man is made of flesh, the baals may be dethroned but never destroyed, and the modern cult of sex and violence is a fresh manifestation of their power. If Elijah had avoided the contest on Carmel, Christianity would perhaps not exist as it does today.

Part 3

WHAT JESUS DID

We have said that Jesus was a superb teacher. He was also a man of action. He involved himself with people in a practical way. Faced with human need he met it, his healing ministry being an important part of that work. Yet he did not perform miracles in order to prove his status, or to draw attention to his message – he had fled from that approach to his ministry when in the wilderness the devil tempted him along those lines.

In any case, witnesses to Jesus's miracles did not inevitably become his followers (see John 11:47ff.). And he himself did not appear to put any great emphasis on them as an aid to faith, as when he said to his disciples, 'Will none of you ever believe without seeing signs and portents?' (John 4:48, NEB), though they did become pointers to who he was. In his Gospel John calls them 'signs'. But primarily his miracles were the expression of his love, acts of his grace, the outflow of his moral excellence.

Jesus performed miracles other than the healing miracles – the so-called 'nature miracles' – the stilling of the storm, the feeding of the five thousand, and so on. That these create problems for some people who can accept the healing miracles cannot be denied. Yet scepticism is misdirected. As C.S. Lewis asked, 'Who, after swallowing the camel of the resurrection, can strain at such gnats as the feeding of the multitudes?'

The central, pivotal act of Jesus was of course his atoning death. That this was *his* act he said himself, 'No one takes [my life] away from me; I am laying it down of my own free will' (John 10:18, NEB). Notice that in the Gospels more space is taken describing the events leading to Jesus's death and the death itself, than to any other aspect of his story. The cross was followed by the resurrection, which was also a great act of God.

58

So the cross and resurrection must be part of this *What Jesus Did* section.

The comments which follow are devotional in character and concentrate on the abiding spiritual significance the works of Jesus have for us today.

THE BOUNDLESS COMPASSION OF LOVE

MARK 1:40–45 – 'Filled with compassion, Jesus reached out his hand and touched the man' (v. 41, NIV).

Healing was not Jesus's top priority, but whenever he was confronted with disease his compassion compelled him to meet the need. There was never any doubt in the leper's mind about Christ's *ability* to heal ('If you are willing . . . you can'); nor was there any doubt in Jesus's mind about his *willingness* to heal ('I am willing'). Yet how can we explain Jesus's words, 'Don't tell this to anyone' unless they mean that Jesus did not want to get too much of a reputation as a healer?

The most significant fact in this passage, however, is one that we can easily overlook. Jesus *touched* the leper. There was no need to touch him to effect physical healing, but Christ's touch would help to heal the outcast's broken spirits. It was not fear of catching the disease that people worried about then for, as a medical consultant to the Leprosy Mission has said, 'You didn't catch it – you inherited it, or you got it as a punishment . . . It was the contamination, rather than the contagion, that they would fear.' It was unthinkable that Jesus, as a religious teacher, should contaminate himself thus. But compassion won the day.

Christians are called to a life of compassion, but it is not the easiest way. As has been said, 'It is . . . much easier to say to a person "go and trust in God alone" rather than to be a faithful supportive friend to someone with problems that seem never ending.'

VICARIOUS FAITH

MARK 2:1–12 – 'Seeing their faith, Jesus said to the paralytic, "My child, your sins are forgiven"' (v. 5, JB).

One interesting aspect of this well-known story is that it was when Jesus saw '*their* faith' that the paralytic man was forgiven. This is thought-provoking, for it most naturally suggests that the sick man was forgiven because of the faith of the four men who, with great ingenuity, had uncovered the roof of the house where Jesus was, to lower their friend on his bed before him. But have we not always been taught that the soul's healing requires the individual's response in faith? We have – and it is true. Jesus normally looked for personal faith in those to whom he ministered.

It was not because of the faith of the four men *alone* that forgiveness came to the sick man. The word '*their*' must have included him also, for a man cannot be forgiven despite himself, without any response on his part. The sick man must also have exercised faith. But the incident does make it clear that the faith of one person may be a contributory factor in another's salvation.

A moment's reflection will show how true this is. Did not the faith of others go a long way into bringing many of us into the Kingdom of God? And is it not the faith of the praying community that so often keeps the wavering Christian on the right road and brings him back when he strays?

Someone said that 'few would be saved if vicarious faith were not effectual for salvation'. The point for us, then, is that it is not sufficient to have exercised personal faith for our own salvation, vital though that is. It is our responsibility also to exercise faith for the salvation of others.

AMONG YOUR OWN FOLK

MARK 5:14–20 – 'Go home to your own folk and tell them what the Lord in his mercy has done for you' (v. 19, NEB).

No longer possessed by a legion of demons and living among the tombs, the man in our reading has now recovered his right mind and is sitting by the lakeside with Jesus. His encounter with Jesus has been so marvellous that it is no wonder he wants to go with him. But Jesus will not permit this – he must go home and tell the people what the Lord has done for him.

No doubt such witness in this area would have been good for the Kingdom; but also, it appears, it would be good for this man! There would be therapeutic value in such action. To be re-established in his own community, and there to bear witness to the change in his life – this would be the best thing that could happen.

Christianity is not a boat trip with Christ to a personal Shangri-La; it is not a convenient escape from the demands of everyday life. Of course, Christ does sometimes call people to 'go with him' to far distant places. But most of us, says Leonard Griffiths, 'he sends back to our familiar world, our home, office, workshop, classroom, community, and he instructs us to talk about him to the people who knew us before we took a religious word on our lips.'

We must think less of escaping from the place where we are, and rather let the words of Christ throw us back into it. This may be what *he* requires of us, and it may be what *we* need.

'SHE ONLY TOUCHED THE HEM'

MARK 5:25–34 – 'She came up behind him in the crowd and touched his cloak, because she thought, "If I just touch his clothes, I will be healed." Immediately her bleeding stopped' (vv. 27–29, NIV).

A study of the healing miracles of Jesus suggests that usually his *words* were sufficient. He touched the little girl, as recorded in Mark 5:41, and she stood up. A similar incident is recorded also in Mark 9:27. He touched the leper (Mark 1:41) – but that was doubtless for psychological reasons. Normally it was a case of, 'Say but the word, thy servant shall be healed' (Albert Orsborn). Here, however, is an incident where a woman 'stole' healing by *touching* Jesus (vv. 28,29), or rather only the edge of his clothing.

Such healing power is not impersonal. Jesus was in such complete control of it that he knew immediately that it had been drawn upon. It was not superstitious magic, nor the woman's audacity, but her *faith* that cured her (v. 34).

As Christians we may be 'the hem of his garment' for people who have neither the boldness nor the opportunity to come initially into direct confrontation with him. The first healing influences may come to them through a 'skirmish' with us. Yet we *need* never fear that such a seeker will be 'let down', for Jesus is immediately aware of their need and their seeking, and confirms and completes the work of grace within them.

Here again we find the value of public confession of Christ, this time *after* healing has taken place. 'Instead of a secret cure, she was given the open benediction of her Lord' (says C.A. Chadwick), and also 'victory over that self-effacing, fearful, half morbid diffidence, which long and weakening disease entails.'

PRAYER IN THE BUSY DAY

MARK 7:31–35 – 'He looked up to heaven and with a deep
sigh said to him, "Ephphatha!" (which means, "Be opened!")'
(v. 34, NIV).

During his busy days Jesus never lost contact with the Father.
Scripture records a number of instances where he looked up to
God (e.g. Mark 6:41). It was a look that revealed the strength
of the link with the Father and his reliance upon him. Although
he was God's Son, he had surrendered his absolute powers when
he came to earth; total manhood meant exactly that for him (see
Philippians 2:7,8).

His obedience and dependence were the key elements in his
success. It is not surprising, therefore, to discover that, as the
pressure increased, he found it necessary to make a brief prayer,
even as he was engaged in his work.

Because there were no barriers between him and the Father he
needed no particular formula of words, or helpful ritual of procedure
to be aware of his link with God. In an instant, even as he looked to
Heaven, the channels of power opened to him.

Some Christians already practise this type of brief, believing
prayer while they are engaged in a demanding task, and have
proved its effectiveness. Hard experience tells us that although we
may have started the day well with prayer, the world has its own
way of influencing and weakening us. Our sensitivity towards God
is lessened as we lose our sense of partnership with him. As the
day wears on and the clamour of our time intensifies, we would
do well to remember that our heavenly Father is but the briefest
of prayers away. Both in preparation for the busy day, and during
it, Christ remains our pattern.

I come, Lord, as a needy soul;
I fail the test of busy days!
I start well, Lord, but lose control
Of time, and harassed are my ways.

DESPAIR AND AMAZEMENT

MATTHEW 8:23–27 – ' "Save us, Lord! . . . We are about to die . . . What kind of man is this?" they said. "Even the winds and the waves obey him" ' (vv. 25,27, GNB).

Compared with the earlier miracles recorded in this Gospel the stilling of the storm is quite different in type. It is a nature miracle, and for many modern readers miracles of this kind cause difficulty because they show Jesus suspending or changing the basic laws of nature. The result has been a search for natural explanations of these events.

Whatever view the reader might take of this miracle, there are some important issues raised in the account of it. The storm was a violent one, so much so that the disciples, some of whom were fishermen and knew the lake, cried out in despair (v. 25). 'Get us out of this somehow', seems to have been the nature of their plea.

The first reaction of Jesus after the disciples had wakened him was not to offer them reassuring words nor yet to still the storm, but to challenge their lack of faith (v. 26). It has been pointed out that these were the significant words at the time the Gospels were written. 'The parallel between the situation of the disciples on the lake and that of the Church in the midst of persecution would naturally suggest itself' (C.E.B. Cranfield).

As amazing as the stilling of the storm, would be the fact that Christ's presence with his people would steady them even when the storms of persecution would not be silenced. That amazing presence is available to us for our lives today.

RESPONSE TO NEED

MATTHEW 15:21–28 – 'Jesus replied, "Woman, what faith you have! Be it as you wish". And from that moment her daughter was restored to health' (v. 28, NEB).

There are some puzzling aspects to this story. At first Jesus refrains from answering the Gentile woman's cry: 'He said not a word in reply.' He also seems to disclaim any responsibility for ministering to Gentiles: He was sent, he said, 'to the lost sheep of the House of Israel'. And when he does address the woman, he appears to speak harshly: 'It is not right to take the children's (ie the Jews') bread and give it to the dogs (Gentiles)'.

In reply to all this we may say confidently that, first, Jesus had no intention of ignoring the woman entirely: we know too much about him to believe that; and eventually he *did* respond positively to her. Perhaps his initial silence was intended to draw out her faith. Then, second, Jesus knew that primarily he must concentrate his ministry on the Jews. Ultimately the whole world was to know of him, for all people are included in God's plan of salvation, but the divine strategy *at this stage* was centred on the Chosen People. And, as to the third point: Jesus's words about not giving the bread to the dogs must have been spoken with a smile and a tone that eliminated any harshness.

What we plainly see here, in spite of the apparent difficulties, is Jesus's reaction to a woman's strong faith (v. 28) and also his own loving response to human need. These two qualities are at the heart of God's dealings with us all: our faith (however small) and his strong love. When these are brought together, there is found the answer to the deepest crying of the human spirit.

CONFIRMATION

MATTHEW 17:1–13 – 'While he was still speaking, a bright cloud suddenly overshadowed them, and a voice called from the cloud: "This is my Son, my Beloved, on whom my favour rests; listen to him"' (v. 5, NEB).

Through Peter, faith in Jesus Christ had been confessed (16:16). It had been a high point in the experience of the disciples. But ever since, it had seemed, nothing but dangers and difficulties had been set before them.

The acclamation of Jesus had hardly been made before Jesus had begun talking of dark and terrible times ahead – for himself and for them. Where then was the Messiah's glory? Where were the joy and victory that belonged to his followers? Perhaps, as sometimes still happens, the initial glow that accompanied the disciples' acceptance of Christ was quickly followed by doubt and confusion, by a gnawing suggestion that it was all a mistake.

But then came the Transfiguration and the doubts were resolved. No escape was provided from the trials ahead, but instead, for one moment, it was granted to Peter, James and John to see Jesus in his glory – *the same Jesus who was leading men to take up their cross*. The truth was confirmed by the Law (Moses) and the prophets (Elijah), and by the voice of God himself. In that moment the three men saw the divine glory shining upon the Lord who, in total dedication, was himself pressing forward with the outworking of his sacrificial life.

For the disciples it was enough. They began to see with new eyes after that. They began to appreciate that God's ways are not man's ways, and that it is the path of service and sacrifice which is illumined with the glory of God, and along which lies the salvation of the world.

FAITH IN THE EVERY DAY

MATTHEW 17:14–21 – 'Afterwards the disciples came to Jesus and asked him privately, "Why could not we cast him out?" He answered, "Your faith is too small . . ."' (vv. 19,20, NEB).

The Transfiguration over, the small company that had been on the mountain 'returned to the crowd' (v. 14), and immediately were confronted by need.

Matthew's account of the incident lays emphasis on the previous failure of the disciples to help – a failure due to their lack of faith (v. 20). It is clear that those who would *follow* Jesus (and following him is now Matthew's theme – cf. 16:24) can do so only as they have faith in the power of God working in them and through them. The idea of moving mountains was a proverbial Jewish expression (cf. 1 Corinthians 13:2); it was accomplished, said Jesus, through faith.

Writing of the descent from the Mount of Transfiguration, Arch R. Wiggins prayed:

> *Unless the glory of the Mount*
> *Be carried to the plain,*
> *Unless we heed the Father's voice,*
> *Our service knows no gain.*

It is Matthew's teaching that the glory of the Mount is not carried to the plain by the endeavour to hold on to and re-create a splendid visible spectacle. The glory is truly transferred in those acts of compassionate and effective action which move mountains, if need be, and which are made possible through a strengthened and continuing faith.

RELIGIOUS ABUSES

MATTHEW 21:12–17 – 'It is written ... My house will be called a house of prayer, but you are making it a den of robbers' (v. 13, NIV).

The temple market was not, in its original concept, an evil institution. It has been estimated that at least two and a half million Jews came to Jerusalem at Passover time. A large proportion of these would be from Jewish settlements abroad. For them to bring animals for sacrifice, and present them at the temple in unblemished condition, would be almost impossible. In addition, the temple tax had to be paid in acceptable coinage, and some means of changing other currency was required. The temple market provided a service which met both of these needs.

The abuses arose out of the extortionate charges which were made for these services. For the exchange service there was an 11 per cent charge, and if the coin offered for exchange was greater in value than the half-shekel required for the tax, a further 11 per cent was charged for giving change. Since the total of 22 per cent represented half a day's wage, this was exploitation indeed – and in the name of religion.

Not all the profits went into the pockets of the traders; some of it went to the temple as freewill offerings. But there can be little doubt that dishonesty did exist (v. 13).

The anger of Jesus was aroused by this exploitation of ordinary people, in the name of religion, for official and personal gain, and the true significance of prayer and worship was forgotten. This is why Jesus turned out the traders. Someone has said that 'he objected to the mingling of man's profit with God's praise'. Religious observance, however important, must not be permitted to get in the way of true worship. 'There is anger at those who exploit the seeker and bar the simple,' wrote William Barclay.

PROFESSION AND PRACTICE

MATTHEW 21:18–22 – 'Seeing a fig-tree at the roadside he went up to it, but found nothing on it but leaves' (v. 19, NEB).

Whatever the difficulties of this story – and they are considerable – the message Jesus wished to convey by the incident is clear enough. Fig-trees had leaves, leaves suggested fruit – but the tree was barren.

This was a symbol of the Israelite people. They professed so much, these people chosen by God and guided by him through the long centuries of their history. They were given privileges far beyond those of other peoples, and far beyond their own deserts. Yet they were condemned in that they had so signally failed to answer God's expectation of them. They promised much and produced nothing.

If this was true of the ancient Jews, it has been true also of a large section of the Christian Church. Again and again God and people have been disappointed in those who, professing so much have produced so little. As William Neil put it in his book, *The Roots of the Radical Theology*: 'Too often in the past two thousand years the worst advertisement for Christianity has been its supporters and advocates.' Oliver Tomkins wrote similarly in *Guarded by Faith*: 'At any given point in the history of the Church, at any given point in an individual life, there is a contradiction between what we are called to be in Christ and what we are in practice.'

He adds, however, 'The contradiction is resolved by faith; that is, by a final and utter trust that God in Christ can make what we are into what we ought to be.'

GIFT FROM THE HEART

MATTHEW 26:6–13 – 'The disciples ... were indignant. "Why this waste?" they asked ... Jesus said ... "Why are you bothering this woman? She has done a beautiful thing to me"' (vv. 8,10, NIV).

Many modern readers of this story will have some sympathy with the complaints of the disciples. According to Mark's account of the incident the perfume was very valuable: 'Three hundred silver coins' (Mark 14:5, GNB), and since a silver coin was a day's wages for an agricultural worker, the perfume was worth about a year's earnings. The disciples were calculating how much good they could have done with the money.

Jesus reminded the disciples, as he reminds us, that an act of true devotion is never carefully calculated. It is a spontaneous expression of one's inner feelings. On a purely human level, many a lover must have spent more than he could afford – certainly more than was prudent – on the beloved, and this because it was the expression of the heart.

The exact intention of the woman is not recorded. Was she anointing Jesus as an expression of her faith that he was the Messiah? If so, Jesus gave the act a more significant meaning. It was preparation for his burial (v. 12). How Jesus must have valued such an open expression of love at a time when hostile forces were gathering around him!

What, then, of the poor who, according to Jesus's own words, we will always have with us? The heart moved with true devotion to Christ cannot be closed to the needs of others. Such a lack of sympathy would be a contradiction of Christian love. The same uncalculating love that prompts our devotion to Jesus prompts our care for those who are in need, and there are always plenty of opportunities to show that love.

GOSPEL FOR THE TOTAL MAN

LUKE 17:11–19 – 'And Jesus said to the man, "Stand up and go. Your faith has made you well"' (v. 19, LB).

There is a puzzling feature about this story. Jesus said to the Samaritan who returned to give thanks, 'Your faith has made you well.' In fact, the other nine were made well also. What can the words of Jesus mean, then, other than that his estimation of human well-being includes but is not limited to the physical?

All ten lepers were healed physically. The Samaritan also entered into a new relationship with Jesus of which his returning to give thanks was the sign. It is this 'new relationship' with Christ, which involves the total person, that is the supreme purpose of the gospel.

The missionary specialist goes out impelled by God's love. As a doctor or a teacher he does not consider his work limited to healing bodies or enlightening minds. It is his fundamental aim to bring Christ himself to those to whom he ministers. This is not to say that the healing ministry and the education programme are *preliminaries* to the preaching of the gospel. They, with the offer of Christ, *are* the preaching of the gospel. A person is not so many parts but a whole – spirit, mind and body – and Christ is concerned with the whole. The Kingdom of God is a breakthrough into the realm of disease and ignorance in body and mind as well as the sin of the spirit.

As we read again this story let encouragement come to us from a contemplation of the complete provision God has made for our good, and let us ask if we are allowing him to do in and through us all he has planned.

THE ONE THING NEEDFUL

LUKE 18:18–27 – 'There is still one thing you lack' (v. 22, LB).

Judged by everyday standards there was little the rich young ruler did not have: youth, wealth, position, security were all his. Moreover he was a man of high ideals and moral stature. He had kept the commandments and striven to live a good life. Yet Christ's judgment of him was that he lacked one thing. It was a vital element, not so much a *thing* as a *spirit*. He did not merely need another virtue adding to his already impressive list – he needed *a whole new approach to life*. He needed to look away from himself, his possessions and his own concerns. That is why Jesus told him to give up his wealth and follow him, involving, on the one hand, *renunciation* and, on the other, *commitment*. He had to find a new centre to his life.

In a television play screened in Britain some time ago Peter and Liz, a young married couple, discovered on their seventh wedding anniversary just how futile life really was for them. They had no centre to their lives outside of themselves and their comfortable suburban home. It was a shattering revelation. Possessing much, they lacked the vital thing, and did not know what it was. Nor did they find it, and the play ended in gloom. It was a mirror to a large slice of twentieth-century living.

Is it not possible for this feeling of disillusion to invade even our religious life? The joy goes from our worship, the vitality from our prayers. This happens when we shift the centre of our concern, if only slightly, from Christ and others to ourselves. It is so easy to do, and it is always fatal. Then the indictment of the rich young ruler applies to us as well.

ALLOWING CHRIST TO SERVE US

LUKE 18:35–43 – '"What do you want me to do for you?"'
(v. 41, RSV).

That there is an important place in our Christian life for service
cannot be denied. There is a whole world of need in which each
of us has to play a part today. This does not, however, as Norman
Pittinger pointed out in his book, *Goodness Distorted*, 'necessarily
mean membership on committees, an Anglo-Saxon substitute, often,
for genuine love. Certainly it does not mean only what in inverted
commas we call "church work", as if being a sidesman or a leader
of the girl guides exhausted Christian discipleship'.

All this may be included, but there is more to Christian experience
than moving around in any kind of activity, however excellent and
outreaching. This is what is implied in Jesus's question to the blind
man, though we are more concerned with asking questions of Christ
than listening while he asks of us. We have our priorities wrong.

What matters first of all is not what we can do for Christ but what
we will allow him to do for us. To quote from Norman Pittinger
again, 'Christian action is that which goes on inside us as we seek
to realise more fully our manhood in and under God.'

Inasmuch as we are willing to be served by Christ with his love
and grace and receive the infilling of his Spirit, shall we 'realise more
fully our manhood in God' and grow towards it. It is a thought for
us all to ponder.

ACTION, NOT SPECULATION

JOHN 9:1–12 – ' "Isn't this the same man who used to sit and beg?" . . . He himself insisted, "I am the man" ' (vv. 8,9, NIV).

For generations the Jews had been preoccupied with the link between sin and suffering. In spite of the protest of the book of Job, all who suffered, and especially those with congenital defects, were seen as being under punishment for some kind of sin. The sight of a man who was blind from birth aroused the spirit of speculation in the disciples and they asked whose sin was responsible for his blindness (v. 2).

Jesus refused to get involved in the argument and dismissed the notion of simple cause of effect altogether. He recognised the fact that the blind man needed compassion and not speculation. Having taken that view, Jesus then showed that this was an opportunity to glorify God by doing God's work 'as long as it is day' (v. 4).

Verses 3 and 4 should be read together, otherwise it is possible to conclude that the man was born blind as a result of God's deliberate action so that divine power could be manifest in Jesus. That kind of philosophy is no better than that of the Jews expressed in verse 2.

The truth is that Jesus, who is 'the light of the world' (v. 5), glorifies God by meeting us at the point of our deepest need. Not all blindness is physical and God has been glorified just as powerfully in the redemption and transformation of human character as in physical healing. Those who have experienced this can join the blind man in his testimony and say, 'I am the man!' (v. 9).

LED TO FAITH

JOHN 2:1–11 – 'This, the first of his miraculous signs, Jesus performed in Cana of Galilee. He thus revealed his glory, and his disciples put their faith in him' (v. 11, NIV).

One of the characteristics of the fourth Gospel is the place given to the miraculous works of Jesus, which John calls 'signs'. John records seven, and the turning of the water into wine is the first of them. At the close of his Gospel John tells us that he has written them down that people may come to believe in Jesus (20:30ff.).

In this Gospel the miracles of Jesus are seen as signs which point to the nature and the character of the One who performed them; and they are, furthermore, symbols and pledges of the blessings which Jesus came to bestow on all mankind. Now this does not do away with the need of people to take the 'step of faith' and place their trust in Jesus; but it is John's prayer that through meditating upon these 'signs', people will find the light of Christ shining into their hearts and illumining for them the Christ, and they will be led to trust in him.

What, then, of this first sign? There can be little doubt but that John saw here that as the water was turned into wine so, in Jesus, Judaism was fulfilled and superseded. The message is that life is transformed through *Christ*; and it is worth noting that this means life in all its aspects. 'His glory', commented Marcus Dods, 'was to be found irradiating all human life.' Jesus first revealed his glory at a wedding feast . . . and people were led to believe in him.

FAITH IN CHRIST

JOHN 4:43–54 – 'Then the father realised that this was the exact time at which Jesus had said to him, "Your son will live." So he and all his household believed' (v. 53, NIV).

The healing of the officer's son is recorded in John's Gospel as the second sign performed by Jesus, and with it a line of thought reaches its conclusion. The cleansing of the temple (2:13ff.) and the discussion with Nicodemus (3:1ff.) showed Jesus as the fulfilment of Judaism; the witness of the woman at Sychar (4:1ff.) showed Jesus meeting the hopes of the Samaritans; and now with this miracle we see the life-giving power of Christ reaching the world of the Gentiles.

It is interesting to observe that here John again portrays a man being led *by stages* to full commitment to Jesus Christ. The officer's first concern was for the welfare of the sick boy, and it was that which took him to Jesus. He pleaded for Jesus to return home with him, but when Jesus told him his son would live, he believed him and on the strength of his words started the journey home.

Here was faith – faith enough to cause the officer to see the transforming power of Christ. But in itself it was not equivalent to making him a believer in Christ. His faith was faith in the truthfulness of the words of Christ and in his readiness and ability to help one in need. It was later, when the immediate need had been met, that the officer followed the implications of what had happened and progressed to further 'faith' in Christ. Having committed his son to the care of the Lord, he committed himself to him. Having believed in Jesus once, he and his household became believers.

CONSTRAINING CIRCUMSTANCES

JOHN 5:1–9 – ' "Do you want to get well?" "Sir," the invalid replied, "I have no-one to help me into the pool" ' (vv. 6,7, NIV).

The crippled man's thoughts of healing centred in the pool by which he sat day after day, yet the lack of people to help him frustrated his every attempt to be healed. But still he sat there – his will almost totally conditioned by his circumstances. When Jesus asked him if he wanted to recover, he replied, 'I have no-one to help me into the pool . . .'

Jesus, for his part, immediately broke through the constraints. His presence alone made a vital difference to the situation, and his command placed a new power within the paralysed man. His intervention made it possible for the man both to triumph over his crippling infirmity and to confound the circumstances which had previously kept him low. The pool, as a means of healing, was not condemned by Christ, but Christ demonstrated his freedom to act without such 'aids' and showed that help and salvation are found in him.

One day in December 1887, when William Booth demanded to know why his followers had not done something to shelter the homeless men of London, valid reasons were quickly forthcoming. Demands were many; workers were few; money was short; and the young Salvation Army could not do everything. But Booth did not care about all that! 'Go and do something,' he ordered. The constraining circumstances remained, but the Spirit of Christ in the life of William Booth insisted that help be given to the needy. And it was. Men moved their beds away from the Thames embankment, and took their first steps towards a better way of life.

OUR GOD CARES

JOHN 11:28–37 – 'When Jesus saw her weeping and the Jews and her companions weeping, he sighed heavily and was deeply moved' (v. 33, NEB).

Other renderings of the phrase, 'he sighed heavily and was deeply moved' (NEB), include, 'He was deeply moved and visibly distressed' (Phillips), and 'He was moved with indignation and deeply troubled' (Living Bible). The phrase 'sighed heavily' is a very strong one, and in some other places in the Gospels is rendered by *indignation* (as in the Living Bible), and may even mean *anger*.

The question arises, therefore: What moved Jesus to indignation, to anger? It has been suggested that he was angry at the scepticism regarding his powers which he found in people around him; that he was angry that people had to suffer so, that death brought such sorrow and heartache. It may be, as Alan Richardson suggested, that his indignation arose because once more a miracle of love would compel him to disclose his Messianic powers and provide yet another reason for his enemies to seek to destroy him. But though we cannot know why he was angry, we do learn from this that he was capable of strong feeling. Again, when he moved near the tomb where his friend Lazarus lay, it is recorded that *he wept*.

If Jesus shows us what God is like, as the New Testament says, then all this means that God is not impassive, compassionless; that he feels for us and takes on his heart our sorrows and pains. We may with confidence take to him our deepest distresses and know that he is able to understand and enter into them with us. Jesus shows us that *our God cares*.

THE DEATH OF DEATH

JOHN 11:38–44 – 'The dead man came out, his hands and feet wrapped with strips of linen, and a cloth around his face. Jesus said to them, "Take off the grave clothes and let him go"' (v. 44, NIV).

In pondering one of the most amazing stories of the New Testament, we have in honesty to admit that difficulties are found here. For one thing, it is surprising that the first three Gospels contain no record of the miracle, which John sees as the chief reason for the Jews' final decision to get rid of Jesus. In the other Gospels the reason for this is the cleansing of the temple.

But whatever the difficulties we feel as we read the story, we cannot deny the vividness of the narrative, an impressive pointer to the authenticity of the happening. In any case, the important thing is not that a dead man was brought to life again – Lazarus had to die eventually – but what the miracle teaches about Jesus. It is this: *he is Lord of life and the conqueror of death*. This does not mean, of course, that believers in Christ escape physical death; this is the one certain thing to which we shall all come. It does mean, however, that death is robbed of its sting; it does not have the power to defeat God's purpose for us. What Jesus demonstrated in Lazarus he was to demonstrate in an even greater way when he himself rose from the tomb.

The last enemy has been conquered, and we may joyfully sing with Percy Dearmer: '*The end of all our way is love, then rise with him to things above – Alleluia!*'

WHERE WAS GOD?

MARK 15:24–39 – 'It was nine o'clock in the morning when they nailed him to the cross' (v. 25, JBP).

In a book by Richard Jeffries a young boy is looking at a picture of Christ's crucifixion. Disturbed by the cruelty of the scene, he turns over the page saying, 'If God had been there he would not have let them do it.' We can sympathise with the youngster. At first sight the cross seems to indict the whole universe of colossal injustice. Where was God when the best man who ever lived died this terrible death? The answer of the Christian Church is 'God was in Christ . . .' This suffering form, impaled upon a Roman gibbet, far from suggesting that God does not care, reveals exactly how much he cares. Here is the measure of God's love. At Calvary we are granted a glimpse into the compassionate heart of God.

The very heart of love is identification. At Calvary God goes to the depths of human suffering and so redeems our human situation from hopelessness.

In the Middle Ages the victims of the plague were cared for by the hermits of St Antony. Without the aid of modern medicine there was little they could do for their patients, but they had one asset. A great artist had painted for them an altar piece of Christ upon his cross and at his burial. It was a terrible picture, powerfully portraying the agony of Jesus. The hermits used to take each patient and lay him on his straw pallet in front of the picture, alone. Many were too ill to notice and some would only be puzzled by it. But a few would glimpse, perhaps for the first time, the truth that God in Christ fully accepted our pain and death.

God was no onlooker at Calvary. He is no mere onlooker when we suffer and struggle.

THANKSGIVING FOR THE CROSS

LUKE 23:32–49 – 'The people stood looking on, and their rulers jeered at him, "He saved others; now let him save himself"' (v. 35, NEB).

The salvation of the world necessitated the death of Jesus. If he would save others he could not save himself. His death was inevitable in the redemptive purposes of God. Not that the sacrifice of the Son was required to propitiate a vengeful Father – that is not the gospel – but that it was God's will that Jesus go on loving, that he never stop loving despite all the evil that could come against him. Jesus would die because, human nature being what it is, his complete and utter loving would lead to his death.

It follows that at one and the same time the Cross reveals, paradoxically, the true nature of sin and the true nature of the divine love. It shows the lengths to which sin can take human kind, for it crucified the Son of God, the 'highest, holiest manhood'. Sin destroys the loveliest and best. It so happened that it was the sins of Pilate, Caiaphas and Judas that sent Jesus to the Cross, but it is a sobering thought that their sins are common to all mankind.

And the Cross reveals the wonder of God's love, for Jesus did go on loving, despite all that was done to him, and his love led to the horrors of Calvary. If this is the extent to which God's love will take him, we can with confidence commit to him our sinful, fearful lives knowing he will receive, forgive and renew us. The Cross is cause for thanksgiving.

HE IS RISEN

MATTHEW 28:1–10 – 'He is not here; he is risen, just as he said. Come and see the place where he lay' (v. 6, NIV).

Christ kept his nerve and God kept his word. Shirking none of Calvary's agony, he fulfilled all the requirements of the sacrificial death which would atone for the sins of the whole world. 'Jesus . . . who for the joy set before him endured the cross, scorning its shame, and sat down at the right hand of the throne of God' (Hebrews 12:2). The world's greatest healer and teacher became the world's only redeemer. His last cry upon the cross was not a cry of anguish, but of triumph (John 19:30). The work of redemption was done.

Because he is God, God kept his word and raised Jesus from the dead. We cannot even imagine the power and skill required to reverse the course of death in a human body. Neither can we imagine the power required to present Christ as the radiant, risen Saviour (Ephesians 1:19,20), a Saviour who was able to overrule the natural laws governing our material world (cf. John 20:19). But God, the Father, used that amazing power in the tomb and, in doing so, turned a terrible defeat into a most glorious victory.

Heaven must have celebrated that glorious moment of resurrection; and slowly, almost unbelievingly, the disciples celebrated Easter Day as it unfolded, until now, today, we celebrate his resurrection with all the heavenly host and with fellow-Christians around the world. What amazing joy is ours! Our sins are gone, our fears dispelled, our hopes are realised! The Lord is risen, and we are alive in him!

> *The powers of death have done their worst*
> *But Christ their legions hath dispersed:*
> *Let shouts of holy joy outburst,*
> *   Alleluia!*
>
> *Symphonia Sirenum Selectarum*

A STORY WITHOUT END

ACTS 1:1–8 – 'In my first book I gave you some account of all that Jesus began to do and teach until the time of his Ascension' (v. 1, JBP).

The gripping story of the Early Church is far more than exciting history. Certainly Luke, who wrote both the third Gospel and the Acts of the Apostles, was a skilful writer and he vividly recreates for us the adventurous beginnings of the Christian community. But it is precisely because he regarded his second volume, not as a story of beginnings, but as a continuation, that it inspires fresh hope in our hearts.

The Gospel was concerned with what Jesus *began* to do and teach, but his work *continued*, after his ascension, through his Church. In every chapter of Acts we sense the ever-present Christ, marching forward to new conquests and claiming fresh territory for his Kingdom.

The implication of this is clear: the story which began in Galilee so long ago is still being written. Christ has not abandoned the world – by his Spirit he is actively at work in it. In a time of confusion like the present, Christians need few things as much as a burning conviction that Christ is working out his purposes. He is our great contemporary, not a historical figure growing more and more irrelevant.

Wrote F.E. Fosdick: 'If one thinks of God only as Father-Creator, he can be a long way off; if one thinks of God only as the Father-Creator revealed in Christ, the historical character, he can be a long way back; but when one perceives God as the Father-Creator revealed in the historic character, and now become the divine Spirit in us, our unseen Friend and abiding Companion, that is an experience to sing about.'

Part 4

THE LIFE OF PRAYER

Prayer is as old as religion and sets humankind apart from the animal kingdom. We have a great deal in common with those non-human creatures who share this planet with us – but in this we are different: we have an awareness of a spiritual dimension to life, an awareness of God, since we were made by him and made like him. This awareness is clearly overlaid in some people by reason of many factors, but in those who believe in and worship God it is real and gives meaning to life.

An important, even central, part of worship is the exercise of prayer. The Bible has a great many striking examples of men and women who prayed and who delighted in prayer. To them prayer was an important part of sharing with God their hearts' needs, their fears and their joys; it was an important part of their coming close to God. There cannot be for any of us a 'coming close', growth in Christlikeness – surely the goal of every Christian – if we neglect our prayer life.

Yet it has been shown by various polls that many, perhaps most, Christians are dissatisfied with their prayer life, and it follows there must therefore be stunted growth and poor communion with God. This must have its result in that dissatisfaction we have been shown is, sadly, so common among Christians. Consequently there must also be a record of ineffective Christian service.

To learn to pray we have *to pray*. No end of looking at other people's prayers alone, no end of reading *about* prayer will make us effective pray-ers. Nevertheless, reading about prayer and perhaps especially looking at other people at prayer, have value in a number of ways: in underlining the importance of prayer; in showing us what prayer should consist of; and also showing us the positive aspects of regular prayer.

85

THE BEST OF WORDS OF LIFE

In this section we are going to look at some of the great prayers of the Bible – from the Old Testament (men like Abraham and Moses knew how to pray) and from the New Testament. We will look especially at the prayers of Jesus and at the guidance he gave to his followers regarding prayer. A man of prayer himself, Jesus is our example *par excellence* in this as in everything good.

THE LIFE OF PRAYER

SILENCE SHARED WITH GOD

MARK 1:32–39 – 'In the early morning, while it was still dark, Jesus got up, left the house and went off to a desert place, and there he prayed' (v. 35, JBP).

Mark begins his Gospel by plunging straight into the Galilean ministry of Jesus. The first chapter moves at such a pace that we can miss the significance of the above-quoted verse. The previous day had been packed with activity. The programme ahead promised to be equally strenuous yet, whereas we would have justified an extra half hour in bed, Jesus rose up very early to pray. To Christ prayer was no duty. It held the promise of glorious renewal.

To pray is to place ourselves consciously in the presence of God. This is far more basic than just thinking *about* God, or speaking *to* God. True friends enjoy each other's presence without the need for continual conversation. Nothing makes for greater unreality in prayer than the idea that fellowship with God depends upon words. Quietly reviewing our lives in the light of eternity, imaginatively holding other people in the love of God – these wordless forms of prayer come more naturally to some than verbal expressions.

When we desire to speak our needs, a quiet pause in God's presence forms the very best preparation. Far better that a few deep longings should emerge from silent waiting upon God, than that words should pour thoughtlessly from our lips.

87

AFFIRMATIVE PRAYER

JOHN 11:38–44 – 'Then they took the stone away and Jesus raised his eyes and said, "Father, I thank you that you have heard me"' (v. 41, JBP).

Describing Christ's action before the grave of Lazarus, Donald (Lord) Coggan wrote, 'The prayer is little more than ejaculatory. Around him is the crowd, critical, inquisitive, grief-stricken . . . He is about to utter the imperatives: "Lazarus, come forth" and "Loose him, and let him go". It is a scene of action. But in the midst of it is a pool of quiet – "Father, I thank thee . . ."'.

Prayer which reaches beyond request to a positive affirmation of God's loving and powerful presence creates for us also a 'pool of quiet' in the midst of turmoil. Lacking this positive note, prayer often becomes a mere rehearsal of anxiety, strengthening the grip of negative emotions upon us. Cleansing is an honest exposure of our negative emotions before God, but we must move on to appropriate God's gifts.

Repeating the same request to God makes prayer weakening instead of strengthening. For instance, many people ask God over and over again to forgive the same failure. Instead, when an old memory haunts us, having once asked God for pardon, we should now say, 'Father, I thank you that you *have* forgiven me.'

Similarly, we should not keep pleading to be delivered from besetting sins. Rather we should pray, 'Lord, thank you that you are working within me, making me more loving, kind, generous, serene and pure.' Of course, some prayer requests cannot be turned into affirmations because we do not know God's will. But prayers for pardon, strength and grace must become affirmations or they will reflect doubt rather than faith.

THE LORD IS OUR KEEPER

MATTHEW 6:9–15 – 'Do not bring us to the test, but save us from the evil one' (v. 13, NEB).

The New English Bible translation is important here. Our Lord is dealing with *the test*, not with temptation to evil, as the Authorised Version suggests, for 'God cannot be tempted with evil and he himself tempts no one' (James 1:13, RSV). The petition is for support in the moral tests that come to moral beings. We are people, not machines, and God has provided power whereby we may come safely through. This is ours when we sincerely seek it.

Without question, our wealthy, materialistic society, with its lowered moral standards is a place of peril for the committed Christian. Not that affluence is evil of itself, of course. There is evil, and inducement to evil, in poverty, and many saintly men and women have felt it their life's work – God's work – to seek to remove it. God made us free to choose good or evil. That this freedom has for many become licence, resulting in a permissive, anything goes kind of society, in no way denies God's wisdom in granting freedom to us. But it does mean that there are particular and peculiar dangers in the world in which we live. That is why the second petition here, to be saved from the evil one, is wholly relevant.

The prayer Jesus gave to his disciples is proof, if we require proof, that all we need is at hand. He would not have taught us to pray this prayer if there were no positive answer to it. We have every good reason to rejoice in his adequate provision.

WHEN TO STOP PRAYING

EXODUS 14:1–18 – 'Then the Lord said to Moses, "Why are you crying out to me? Tell the Israelites to move on"' (v. 15, NIV).

Commenting on this passage, G.A. Chadwick asks what at first sight might be considered a strange question: Can prayer ever be out of place? And he answers, 'Not if we mean a prayerful, dependent mental attitude towards God. But certainly, yes . . . if our own duty has to be done, and we pass the golden moments in inactivity, however pious.' There is a time to pray and there is a time to stop praying and get on with the work.

It was such a time in the history of the Israelites. They were trapped; behind them the Egyptian army; in front of them an impassable sea. What was to be done? They 'clamoured to the Lord for help' (v. 10, NEB), and then turned upon Moses, expressing bitter regret that they had ever listened to him and allowed themselves to be led out of Egypt. Better slavery than death, they moaned. Moses' reaction was typical of him: he turned to the Lord. The answer he received to his prayer – 'Stop praying and start moving' – was probably unexpected, but he passed it on to his people.

Now, our own prayers are but meaningless mumblings if we are able to answer them ourselves. What is the point of crying to God if we are neglecting to use the commonsense and energy he has given us? There is never any fear that he will not or cannot help us. When, having reached the end of our resources, we stand helpless before him, he will come to our aid. But with respect to some of our problems – more, perhaps, than we imagine – he may be saying: no more talking, start doing something about this yourself. Then it is industry and holy determination that we need.

TEACH US TO PRAY

JOHN 17:6–19 – 'I pray for them' (v. 9, NIV).

In this, the second of the three sections of his prayer (the others are vv. 1–5 and vv. 20–26), Jesus prays earnestly for his disciples. They are to be exposed to the attacks of 'the world' without the presence of their Master.

'I pray for *them*,' says Jesus and emphasises that his prayer is not for the world. This does not mean that he has no concern for the plight of those who are far from God; the prayer does not forget the mission of the Church (see vv. 18 and 23). But now it is *the believers* who are in need of God's strengthening. 'I *pray* for them,' William Temple translated as, 'I ask concerning them,' and stresses that here the tone is far from stern demand and more a sharing of concern. Throughout this prayer, Jesus does not batter the heart of God but imparts to his Father his deep longings for his friends.

Although there are times when we need to entreat God in our prayers, sometimes our faith must show itself in less 'violent' prayer. When Salvationist missionaries saw the great door of China close behind them, they too were 'going away' and leaving behind a lonely group of believers. Yet it was with an air of supreme confidence in an all-powerful God that they were able to sing prayerfully for their comrades, 'Strong the hand stretched forth to shield us, All must be well' (Mary Peters).

We, too, must allow the nature of our intercessions to arise from the depth of our trust in a loving God.

PRAYER IN THE UPPER ROOM

MARK 14:22–26 – 'While they were eating, Jesus took bread, gave thanks and broke it' (v. 22, NIV).

In these all too brief verses we sense the atmosphere of gratitude and devotion in which our Lord lived. Sandwiched, as they are, between Jesus's prophecy of Judas' betrayal and of the flight of the other disciples, 'it is a story radiant with praise and thanksgiving'.

In view of the brevity of the Gospels it is surprising the number of times in which we read of Jesus giving thanks for bread. Clearly, it was his habit to say 'grace before meals' and in this – as in all else – he is our example.

Vincent Taylor suggested that his 'grace' probably took the following form of words: 'Praise be thou, O Lord our God, King of the universe, who bringest forth bread from the earth,' or 'Blessed art thou, our Father in Heaven, who givest us today the bread necessary for us.' When we consider what the next few hours would entail for our Lord, we cannot but marvel.

The meal finished, they sang a hymn – on the strength of which he went out to face calumny, torture and cruel death. May our devotional life be of the quality to strengthen us in the face of such opposition and pain as may be our lot!

> *Must Jesus bear the cross alone,*
> *And all the world go free?*
> *No, there's a cross for everyone,*
> *And there's a cross for me.*

PRAYER IN TIMES OF GRIEF

JOHN 11:33–44 – ' "Where have you laid him?" he asked. "Come and see, Lord," they replied. Jesus wept' (v. 34, NIV).

Why did Jesus grieve? Many factors may have moved him so deeply: sympathy with the sorrowing Martha and Mary; the unbelief of those standing around; the feeling that one so young as Lazarus should have died. These are but speculations.

But grief drove him to prayer. No such burden need be borne unaided, for the heavenly Father waits to share his children's sense of loss. Physical withdrawal in this instance was impossible, and often is for us.

But we can always withdraw into ourselves – and there find God.

> *Prayer is the burden of a sigh,*
> *The falling of a tear,*
> *The upward glancing of an eye*
> *When none but God is near.*

Even in a crowd we can feel that 'none but God is near'. The 'secret place of the Most High' may be the busy market and the thronged highway. Jesus found this to be so.

The Father is present, he is listening, and Jesus is in touch with him. Because of this, all is well. Victory is assured; death must give way to life. Let us remember in prayer the bereaved, that they may be comforted; and let us pray for ourselves, that we might have the gift of sympathy.

PRAYER IN TIMES OF JOY

LUKE 10:17–24 – 'Jesus, full of joy through the Holy Spirit, said, "I praise you, Father, Lord of heaven and earth,"' (v. 21, NIV).

We are reaching a measure of spiritual maturity when all the varied experiences of life are linked immediately with the life of devotion. In our last comment we saw how grief drove our Lord to prayer, and perhaps we have found this to be true in our own experience – God is the bringer of comfort in times of distress. But the above reading shows us Jesus immediately sharing his joys with the heavenly Father, and this may not come so naturally to us.

Are we not tempted in our delights to forget the Giver of every good and perfect gift? Sadly, many of us may have to admit this to be true. Too rarely do we spontaneously turn to God and say, 'I thank you, Lord of heaven and earth.'

Someone who knew that too little of our prayer is given up to praise wrote to a friend on holiday: 'Do you know, I think one of the best things you can do on holiday is to ask nothing, want nothing, but just praise God for everything? . . . Just utter one long praise for little beautiful things and forget the great, big, striving, blundering self of yours. Then come back clean and fresh and let us, too, get a sight of the glory of God.'

All praise and thanks to God
The Father now be given,
The Son and him who reigns
With them in highest heaven . . .
    Martin Rinkart
    (*trs Catherine Winkworth*)

THANK GOD

1 CORINTHIANS 1:3–9 – 'I always thank God for you because of his grace given you in Christ Jesus' (v. 4, NIV).

Prayers of affirmation and prayers of thanksgiving are closely related. Note how in this Scripture reading praise merges into confidence. If thanksgiving is a dominant note in our prayer life negative attitudes will not long persist.

Thanksgiving may sometimes be spontaneous – and sometimes it needs to be deliberate. Mother Julian of Norwich noted that: 'Sometimes, for plenteousness, it breaketh out with voice and saith: "Good Lord, I thank thee. Blessed mayest thou be."' At other times, 'when the heart is dry and feeleth not, then it is driven by reason and by grace to call upon our Lord with voice, rehearsing his blessed Passion and his great goodness.'

Rehearsing the causes for thanksgiving in our lives is not a dishonest pretence of gratitude we do not feel. It is an attempt to see life in perspective, to escape the narrow preoccupations which make us ungrateful.

Thanksgiving is not without its dangers. When it focuses only upon our health, good fortune, success it may encourage the illusion that we are one of God's specially favoured ones. Thanksgiving, as well as petition, needs a broader reference than our own. It should include God's bounty to all mankind, and the goodness we see in other lives.

Wrote Dr William Sangster: 'Thank God for common blessings: for the harvest fully gathered in and the great moon rising above; for the sudden smile of a friend met unexpectedly in a place where you did not expect to meet anyone you knew; thank God for home . . . for the loyalty of family . . . for all ordinary things, taken for granted when they ought to be taken with gratitude. Thank God! Thank God!'

PRAYER AND THANKSGIVING

LUKE 22:13–20 – 'Jesus and his apostles reclined at the table. And he said to them, "I have eagerly desired to eat this Passover with you before I suffer"' (vv. 14,15, NIV).

Even in the most difficult situations Jesus never ceased to be positive; nor did he cease to be thankful. With the suffering of Calvary drawing nearer by each painful, hurrying moment, Jesus still eagerly anticipated his last Passover with his disciples. With amazement we also note that when he took the cup, which was symbolic of his shed blood, he did so with thanks (vv. 17,20). In the same spirit of thanksgiving he took the bread and broke it as a symbol of the imminent breaking of his own body. From the example of his Master, Paul wrote to the Philippians, 'In everything, by prayer and petition, with thanksgiving present your requests to God' (Philippians 4:6).

Thanksgiving is a crucial element in prayer. By our expressed gratitude to God we affirm our awareness that we are totally safe in his hands. Thankfulness is easy when life is untroubled, but the test of our love is whether or not we can be thankful when the way is hard. To members of her prayer group Evelyn Underhill wrote, 'There is and will be suffering for all of us. There are only two ways of taking suffering. We can resist or hate it, or we can accept it as a privilege and thank God for it.' That, surely, is in the Spirit of Jesus.

Not only does thanksgiving help us to put events into their true perspective, it also lifts the spirit. Our natural inclinations are towards self-pity and complaint. We look at others who appear unpressured and tend to question God's providential care. But when the spirit of thanksgiving takes over, we can count our many blessings.

> *For ease which comes swift after pain,*
> *For peace which follows after strain,*
> *For seeming loss now turned to gain,*
> *I thank thee, Lord.*
>
> *Doris Rendell*

PRAYER AND PETITION

LUKE 11:9–13 – 'So I say unto you: Ask and it will be given to you; seek and you will find; knock and the door will be opened to you. For everyone who asks receives' (vv. 9,10, NIV).

Since God has chosen to be known to us by the name of Father, it follows that he is looking for an ideal 'Father and child' relationship between us. Clearly, a child's dependence means that requests of one kind or another are inevitable and God, says Jesus in this Scripture, is only too willing to hear our requests and to answer them. Petition, therefore, is another essential element in prayer. The encouragement to 'pray continually' (1 Thessalonians 5:17) carries with it the willingness of God to receive and respond to our requests.

One of our problems regarding petitioning God is that we feel our appeals are unreasonable, as though God cannot answer because he has locked himself into the laws of creation and is unable to move freely within those laws, or even to transcend them. Perhaps we should let God be the best judge of that and still make our petitions in faith. Our Lord's promises are quite staggering! If we are going to do greater things than he did we are left with no alternative but to make big prayers and to make them in his name (John 14:12,13).

'You do not have, because you do not ask,' said James and, 'When you ask, you do not receive because you ask with wrong motives' (James 4:2,3). We can be sure the request we make that is not consistent with the mind of God will not be granted, and some genuine requests will appear to be unanswered because God's timetable is different from ours, or because he will answer another way. But, although our petitions are meant to include the ordinary issues of life, the truth stands – our prayers can be the opportunity we give to God to make us Christlike, and to use us in ways we could not even imagine.

CHRIST OUR PATTERN

LUKE 9:18–20 – 'Once when Jesus was praying in private and his disciples were with him' (v. 18, NIV).

Our Lord's ability to pray in private while surrounded by his disciples reflects the naturalness of his prayer life. Presumably his preference was to pray in solitude but prayer could not be deferred until the occasion was right: any time is the right time, and anywhere is the right place. There was no division between the Christ at work and the Christ at prayer. It is a standard to which we aspire since he is our example.

Prayer for Jesus was part of his dynamic relationship with God. Not for him the dryness and dullness which sometimes marks our prayer life. By prayer he was linked with God in all his majesty and grace. This ensured that God's strategy and enabling power dominated his life. Danger there might be, but dullness – never! Prayer was an essential dynamic in his lifestyle.

As we consider the separate strands of prayer we must not omit the important element of confession. This is possible when we take Christ as our pattern since he, being sinless, had no sins to confess. But this is not so with us. We are still striving, in John Keble's perceptive words, 'to live more nearly as we pray'. When we pray we confess our failure to take the grace that makes us strong, to live up to our potential; and we confess our sins. Then, having received forgiveness we pledge ourselves to a more faithful expression of the call to Christlikeness he has given us.

THE LIFE OF PRAYER

'YOUR WILL BE DONE'

MATTHEW 21:28–32 – 'He . . . said, "Son, go and work today in the vineyard." "I will not," he answered, but later changed his mind and went' (vv. 28,29, NIV).

Many of us may make the prayer, 'Your will be done' (Matthew 6:10) a daily petition, but it is good to ask ourselves what difference this makes to our day to day living. Much depends on the tone in which the prayer is said. Is it a prayer of resignation, to the unavoidable? Or is it a glad and wholehearted assent to the doing of that apart from which life is a disaster?

Do we say 'Amen' to God's purpose for ourselves? It is pointless deploring the waywardness of others, or the sorry plight of mankind at large, unless we are declaring by word and life that we are one hundred per cent with God in the carrying out of his intentions.

Salvationist hymn writer John Lawley penned the words:

> Thy will and wish I know are for the best,
> This gives to me abundant peace and rest.

If this is true – and theoretically at least we consent to it – there should be a full and glad acceptance of his will. Too often we give way to God only because we cannot help doing so, and therefore the note of joyous abandon is missing from our religion.

Part of the teaching of the parable noted above is simply that what we *do* is more important than what we *say*. One son said 'Yes' to his father – then pleased himself. The other said 'No' – then repented his disobedience and made amends. Perhaps this is God's word for us. 'Your will be done' – this is a battle-cry. To act upon it is to find personal victory. Let us lift up our hearts!

POWER FOR SERVICE

ACTS 4:23–31 – 'At their prayer the place of meeting was shaken, and they were all filled with the Holy Spirit, speaking God's word fearlessly' (v. 31, JM).

Visiting in his Glasgow parish, Arthur Gossip came late in the afternoon to the threshold of a five-storey tenement where a parishioner lived on the top floor. Tired and inwardly weary, he said to himself, 'I've had enough. I'll come tomorrow.' Then it seemed to him that a presence brushed passed him with the words, 'Then I shall have to go alone.' This was sufficient to take Gossip through the doorway and, strangely strengthened, he mounted the stairs.

Fellowship with God immeasurably increases our resources for living and serving. Threatened by persecution, the disciples urgently prayed for power to witness. The tremendous reinforcement of the Spirit was theirs immediately. Like the Glasgow minister, they wanted, not to bask in a sense of their own adequacy, but to be adequate for others.

Prayer brings power proportionate to our need, never in excess of our commitment. If we withhold ourselves from self-giving we never know the full measure of God's empowering. 'Prayers that has no need in 'em,' said a rustic philosopher, 'has no suction power.' This is as true of need in those we want to help as of our own needs.

God's strengthening awaits our response to others and also leads to further self-giving. This is why the normal Christian experience is not one of *feeling* strong but of God's grace made perfect in weakness.

Jeremy Taylor prayed: 'Jesus Christ, who hast given thy life to redeem me, thyself for my example, thy word for my rule, thy grace for my guide, thy body on the Cross for the sin of my soul: enter in and take possession of my heart, and dwell with me for ever.'

THE LIFE OF PRAYER

PRAYER FOR ALL OF THEM

JOHN 17:18–21 – 'My prayer for all of them is that they will
be of one heart and mind, just as you and I are, Father' (vv.
20,21, LB).

Christ's prayer is so personal, so deep, so powerful, that any
comment on it is bound to be a poor substitute for personal
meditation on the prayer itself. All that a commentator can do
is stress that Christ's prayer must be taken seriously. His demand
for unity among Christians, like the unity there is between himself
and his Father, cannot be taken lightly. We must work with and
worship with other Christians, even with those whose understanding
is different from our own, if the unity for which Christ prayed is to
be shown to the world.

Christ consecrated himself to meet *our* need for growth in truth
and holiness – not just the need of his early disciples, not just the
need for a few selected Christians with special gifts for holiness, not
just the need of ministers, pastors, teachers or preachers, members
of one denomination or another. Christ's consecration meets the
need of all future believers (v. 20).

We all share in Christ's consecration. Our sacrifice, our dedication,
our work, our witness, our unity with other Christians, are all a part
of that single-minded consecration of Christ. He gave himself for
others and expects us, in unity, to do the same.

Christ's example shows how one person's consecration and obedience can affect countless others. Our consecration and obedience,
too, may affect the lives of other people.

COUNTDOWN FOR SODOM

GENESIS 18:22–33 – 'Abraham approached the Lord and asked, "Are you really going to destroy the innocent with the guilty? If there are fifty innocent people . . . will you destroy the whole city? . . . You can't do that . . . The judge of all the earth has to act justly"' (vv. 23–25, GNB).

This is the first biblical example of intercession. Noah had watched the inundation of his world without a word of pity for his contemporaries, but now, when the flood is a lava rather than water, Abraham tries to persuade God to be true to his nature as 'judge of all the earth' and not destroy the innocent with the guilty. His argument is still valid: 'If you can't differentiate between the guilty and the innocent, you ought to assume that all are innocent rather than that all are guilty.'

We should not think that Abraham was really changing God's mind by this 'Dutch auction' procedure. God's attitude was already one of love and mercy, but he already knew that there weren't ten good people in Sodom. So each time Abraham utters his prayer God's answer is a 'Yes, if'. The 'if' is essential if God is to remain true to his nature. Good parents do not always say 'Yes', but often 'Yes, if', and we should never expect an unconditional surrender from God.

Is there any point, then, in praying for others if we cannot change God's mind? Yes, for Abraham's prayers did *him* good if they did not help the city dwellers. They were part of his spiritual education, and they identified him with God's desire to redeem his people. We have since learned more – that natural disasters are not coincidental with punishment for sin, but Abraham's gropings for truth help us to realise that God's nature is love and mercy – in spite of appearances.

PRAYER FOR HEALING

MARK 2:1–12 – ' "But that you may know that the Son of Man has authority on earth to forgive sins . . ." He said to the paralytic, ". . . take your mat and go home!" ' (vv. 10,11, NIV).

A London vicar received an urgent phone call from a man who had been told he had an incurable disease. Faced with this startling verdict the man now deplored his careless neglect of spiritual issues. The vicar placed the man's name, and that of his wife, on his intercession list, but suggested that prayer would be more fruitful if the couple learned to pray. An appointment was eagerly made. Later the vicar received a telephone message: 'No, padre, I'm glad to say I won't be troubling you after all.' Apparently the earlier diagnosis had been changed to one less serious. The patient's desire to learn to pray had evaporated with his fears.

Prayer for healing is sometimes suspect because people imagine it encourages this attitude. God should never be treated as a *means* to bodily health, although it must be added that most of us seek God for quite selfish motives. Rightly understood, the Church's ministry of healing aims at wholeness of spirit, mind and body. It also recognises that God uses many means – medicine, psychiatry, community concern, friendship and prayer – to make people whole.

In praying for the sick we do just what the friends did for the paralytic in this reading. We set those for whom we pray in the presence of Christ. Imaginatively, we may picture his hand outstretched upon them. We neither restrict his purpose to physical cure, nor set limits upon what Christ can accomplish.

PRAYER MAKES THINGS HAPPEN

ACTS 1:9–14 – 'They all joined together constantly in prayer, along with the women and Mary the mother of Jesus, and his apostles' (v. 14, NIV).

From their last meeting with Jesus on the Mount of Olives near Jerusalem, the disciples returned to the upper room in the city to await the fulfilment of the promise. If the twentieth-century Church is going to rediscover the fact and power of the Holy Spirit it would do well to notice the first disciples' preparation to receive him. They prayed in a spirit of expectancy.

When God's people pray, things happen! Our ineffectiveness, corporate and individual, is surely in part a pointer to the poverty of our prayer life: it is certainly not an indication of the unwillingness or inability of God to work in and through us. 'I have little time to pray', we say so often and, though we have more leisure time than ever before, we actually believe it. Perhaps it is not so much the *time* we lack, as the *desire*, because 'the world is too much with us'.

We live in hectic days – bustle and excitement are all about us. So much is happening and, with modern means of communication, we are made aware of it very quickly, often now as it happens. People are losing the art of being still and we Christians are conditioned by this atmosphere. But if prayer is as vital as the New Testament indicates – *and it is* – we cannot afford to neglect it.

HONEST PRAYERS

PSALM 109:21–31 – 'Help me, O Lord my God; save me in accordance with your love' (v. 26, NIV).

The first part of this psalm – which some may wish to read in addition to the verses noted above – contains either the imprecations of the psalmist against his enemies or, as some think, the psalmist's quotation of the curses used against him by those who hate him. In either case it is not the most elevating kind of reading.

If they are the psalmist's own words they are far removed from the spirit of true religion, as New Testament teaching shows, and they indicate again how even good people may fall below God's standards. Condemn him for his loveless expressions, but commend him for pouring out his resentments and not brooding over them. He felt vengeful (which was not to his credit) but he took his feelings to God (which was).

Pretence is no firm basis for prayer; surely God wants us to be honest as we pray. When we feel bitter about someone is not the time to refrain from prayer, but the very time to pray, making the bitterness the subject of our prayer. We sing, in the words of the old hymn:

> *Do thy friends despise, forsake thee?*
> *Take it to the Lord in prayer . . .*

And it is also right, when we are the despiser, to take *that* fact to the Lord in prayer.

It was right for the psalmist to invoke God's help against the wickedness of his enemies. And we may be sure that our own prayers for protection against the assaults of evil will not go unheard. We are always safe in the unfailing love of God.

POLITICS AND PRAYER

MARK 8:27–38 – 'He asked them, "Who do people say I am?"
. . . Peter replied "You are the Christ"' (vv. 28,29, NIV).

If Jesus used the term Son of Man more than any other in respect
to himself – as the Gospels show – the title Christ, or Messiah, was
seldom on his lips. It occurs many times in the New Testament, of
course – fifty-five in the Gospels alone – but Jesus was reluctant
to use it himself. This was not because he disclaimed the right to
it. On the contrary, as this reading shows, when others confronted
him directly with the question of his acceptance of the title, he
clearly acknowledged that he was the Christ. But he was reluctant
to use the term himself because of the political and nationalistic
ideas associated with it in his own day.

He *was* that Christ, but not the Christ of Jewish expectations.
His kingdom, as he told Pilate (John 18:36) was not of this world.
This does not mean, for us, that we should have nothing to do with
the affairs of this world, that we stand aside from political and social
questions and preach a 'purely spiritual' gospel, as some Christians
have sometimes mistakenly imagined. It is our Christian duty to get
involved in those areas of life.

But Jesus's concept of his mission as the Christ means that
our concern must not relate to the building of a society solely
in material and physical terms. These are important, but we see
them in their context in the total life of men and women, where
politics and prayer are – or should be – all of a piece.

SOME DIFFICULTIES ON THE WAY

LUKE 18:1–8 – 'Jesus told his disciples a parable to show them that they should always pray and not give up' (v. 1, NIV).

'I throw myself down in my chamber,' wrote the seventeenth-century poet John Donne, 'and I call in, and invite God and his angels thither, and when they are there I neglect God and his angels, for the noise of a fly, for the rattle of a coach, for the whining of a door.' How typical is this experience in all who have tried seriously to pray! And when outward distractions are mercifully absent there often remains an inner turmoil even more difficult to combat.

Another major discouragement in prayer is the feeling of sheer boredom, or dryness which sometimes sweeps over us. Keith Miller says that in much of his life he had been a 'spiritual sensualist', always wanting to *feel* God's presence in prayer and depressed when he didn't. 'I saw that until I could believe without spiritual goose pimples I would always be vacillating,' he writes, 'and my faith would be at the mercy of my feelings.'

Until we recognise that prayer is conducted at the level of the will, distractions and moods will always worry us. Once we have grasped this truth we see that a prayer persisted in, despite all rebellious thoughts, is better evidence of the Godward direction of our will than a less costly prayer. Similarly, we shall recognise how little our emotional state has to do with the essential business of communion with God.

WHEN THE ANSWER IS 'NO'

MARK 14:32–38 – '"Dear Father," he said, "all things are possible to you, please – let me not have to drink this cup. Yet it is not what I want but what you want"' (v. 36, JBP).

Asked if God had answered her prayer a little girl instantly replied, 'Yes, he said "No".' In addition to this simple trust we need to see that what we call 'unanswered prayer' is a challenge to our intelligent inquiry.

Is our prayer 'unanswered' because we failed to cooperate with God? 'God is no respecter of persons,' wrote John Gaynor Banks, 'but he is a respecter of conditions. We must learn to supply these conditions more effectively.' Asking God for better health while ignoring simple rules of diet or hygiene, praying to be delivered from resentment while making no expression of goodwill, requesting serenity while maintaining an overcrowded programme – this kind of prayer treats God as a magician.

Is prayer 'unanswered' because we are enmeshed in the total situation of human sin and rebellion? Even Jesus could do no mighty works in Nazareth 'because of their unbelief'. Much prayer which is according to God's will nevertheless fails its *primary* objective for similar reasons. We can, however, believe that genuine prayer never leaves a situation entirely as it was.

John Magee believes prayer is best focused 'on those aspects of existence which are dynamic and growing, the turning points or growing edges of life'. The physical universe, for instance, is not an area for prayer action but rather the firm stage upon which our lives are acted out. This may be a further reason why, to some prayers, the answer is 'No'.

DELIGHT IN GOD

JOHN 20:26–29 – 'Thomas said to him, "My Lord and my God"' (v. 26, NIV).

A triangle with one side left out was Baron von Hugel's description of religion which ignores the adoration of God. This would present no problem if adoration flowed from our hearts as spontaneously as it did from Thomas when he met the risen Christ. In any life these moments are rare. What we need, if adoration is to give depth and vision to our prayers, is what one writer described as 'a sustained intention to worship'. Without this, prayer easily becomes a chatty monologue with a god we create in our own image.

As noted in a previous comment in this section, prayer begins best with, and arises out of, a silence shared with God. Next, we should look away from ourselves to God. This is adoration. Since we can never see or imagine God as he is in himself, we can be helped by flashing upon the screen of our minds a picture embodying some facet of God's being. Imaginatively we recall a beautiful landscape, the immensities of space, a saintly character, the sheer mystery that we *are*, an episode from the Gospels. Each can lead us to adore God, and a little forethought will prevent monotonous repetition.

This selfless delight in God which is adoration does more to release us from egotism, and heal our wounds, than much self-recrimination. This all the masters of prayer affirm.

SURPRISED AT THE ANSWER

ACTS 12:5–17 – 'So Peter was kept in prison, but the Church was earnestly praying to God for him' (v. 5, NIV).

This story underlines the importance of praying with faith. The company gathered in the house of Mary were praying for Peter, who was in prison. When Peter was released and knocked at the door, they could not believe their ears and eyes. It has been suggested that they obviously prayed with little expectation of an answer. But need that be so? We are not told that they prayed for Peter's release; perhaps their faith did not extend to this. They had prayed *for Peter*. Far from that being evidence of *little* faith, it does in fact suggest that they had a large understanding of prayer.

It is a sign of spiritual maturity to pray, not for the lifting of a burden or the changing of circumstances, but for the person concerned, that he may have the strength to endure. So with ourselves: it is better to pray for grace to bear the trial than to pray for the trial to be removed.

There is a corollary to this interpretation of the incident. It is this: sometimes we have to take for granted the answer to our prayers. We may have no consciousness of any kind of change in us or in those for whom we have prayed, *but it may have happened anyway*. The answer has been given though we may not see it for a long time. It often takes time before we appreciate the beauty and meaning of a painting or a piece of music. Similarly, we may not immediately appreciate the answer, the *right* answer, to our prayer *which was given as we prayed*.

Part 5

SPOKESMEN FOR GOD

We noted earlier that there is a class of men in the Old Testament whose greatness lay in their remarkable insight into the ways and purposes of God, and their readiness to interpret those truths to the people at whatever cost. They are called the 'writing' prophets since there is a book written by or about them.

Prophecy didn't start with them, of course. The prophetic movement in Israel goes back to very early times. But these 'writing' prophets are in a category of their own. For one thing, there is on record more of what they said than earlier prophets such as Moses, Nathan, Elijah and others had to say. And their messages were a development of earlier teaching, and represent the high points of Old Testament theology.

Indeed, there is a development within the corpus of the writing prophets themselves, though this can be seen only if we arrange the books into their chronological order. They appear to have been given their place in Scripture more on account of their length than anything else!

Isaiah is placed first, followed by the other longer books, Jeremiah and Ezekiel. In point of time Amos was first. The longer books are referred to as the 'major' prophets, and the shorter as the 'minor' prophets. It should be kept in mind that 'major' and 'minor' refer not to quality but to quantity.

We have to be full of admiration for these outstanding men. They had a remarkable insight into God's purposes, as we have said. They maintained unswerving loyalty to God whatever the circumstances. They had unbounded determination to speak for him, even when their words were unpalatable to their hearers, as often they were, and even when they provoked violent opposition, as sometimes they did.

They were truly great men, and we can learn a great deal from

111

them still, today. Speaking centuries before Christ they nevertheless uttered words that have power to hearten and challenge us. Of course their message was limited. It couldn't be otherwise. Jesus had not yet come; the full revelation had not yet been given. So ultimately we turn from them to him. But they speak to our hearts today, as the following comments undoubtedly show.

GOD AND HUMAN RESPONSIBILITY

AMOS 1:1,2 – 'The words of Amos, one of the shepherds of Tekoa – what he saw concerning Israel' (v. 1, NIV).

It is often pointed out that the cry of the Old Testament prophets was, 'Thus says the Lord', that their message was direct from God and that they were not propounding their own opinions and theories. And this is true, but requires the qualification brought out by J.B. Phillips in his illuminating rendering of Amos 1:1: '. . . when *he saw the truth* about Israel'.

The prophet was not a piece of machinery, a microphone God switched on when he had something to say. He was an interpreter of God's will in a situation he himself was observing and, indeed, in which he himself lived. In a brilliant short study of the prophet Amos, Gerhard von Rad says, 'We see a man's vitality and intellectual acumen at work . . . the contribution made by his own alert mind must not be underrated.'

This emphasises God's respect for human personality, his recognition of the contribution each person may make individually to the on-going cause of the gospel. People who answer the call of Christ and commit themselves to him without reserve, do not become heaven-sent automatons, having abrogated the faculty of independent thought and critical judgment. Each person is and remains a *unique* being, in the true sense of that word, in full possession of a God-given freedom which can be exercised in the joyful discharge of his or her particular responsibility.

That God is able to reveal himself *to* and *through* all the varied expressions of human personality is a truth both challenging and heartening.

SANDWICH-BOARD THEOLOGY

AMOS 4:12,13 – 'Prepare to meet your God, O Israel. He who forms the mountains . . . and reveals his thoughts to man . . . the Lord God Almighty is his name' (vv. 12,13, NIV).

'Prepare to meet your God' has been the message on many a religious sandwich-board, which is a pity because, if we can say only five words about God, they should not be those words. We would be better to settle for three: 'God is love'. Not that there is no place in Christianity for the fearsome threat of judgment, but that is only part of the story and gives a distorted view of God if separated from the rest.

The threat of judgment is God's last resort in his dealings with us. It is only after statements of love and appeals for repentance and warnings galore that he has to say, 'This is what I will do to you' (v. 12). Our theology of judgment must always be an appendix to our theology of God's love and our salvation through Christ, not just a preface to a religion of fear and guilt.

It is important, however, to notice that the verse originally applied to the nation's meeting her fate in history, rather than to individuals meeting their judgment in eternity. James Hastings wrote: 'Men make a great mistake in supposing that the only meeting with God for which they are to prepare is that compulsory meeting with him in the day of judgment.' We need to prepare daily for our meetings with him, for he is not only the distant God of *creation* (who 'forms mountains, creates wind'); he is the immediate God of continuous and progressive *revelation* (who 'reveals his thoughts to man', v. 13).

UNACCEPTABLE LUXURY

AMOS 6:1–7 – 'Woe to you who are complacent in Zion, and you who feel secure on Mount Samaria . . . You lie on beds inlaid with ivory . . . you drink wine by the bowlful . . . but you do not grieve over the ruin of Joseph' (vv. 1,4,6, NIV).

The luxurious lifestyle of the rich had already been exposed by Amos – 4:1 – but the theme receives more comprehensive treatment in this reading. Most of the prophet's words were directed against the Northern Kingdom, but he now considers the whole of God's chosen people, Judah as well as Israel, and the capital cities of both Kingdoms are named in verse 1.

People in Jerusalem were no better than their counterparts in Samaria. They were complacent lovers of luxury. Examples of furniture inlaid with ivory were found during archaeological excavations at Samaria in 1938. These probably date from the time of Amos and help to confirm the prophet's observations on the lifestyle of the wealthy members of society. Amos presents a picture of idleness, revelry and self-indulgence. There was feasting, singing, drinking wine by the bowlful, but no thought of the impending ruin of a nation which ignored the needs of its yeoman classes.

Sins of luxury and indulgence often accompany affluence. The prophet's love of justice was incensed by what he saw, and he concluded that God, who is perfect holiness, must abhor the unrighteous behaviour of his people. In an age when we are given a world rather than a parochial vision, what has the prophet to say to the luxury loving sections of our world when millions starve?

WORDS WITHOUT HEART

HOSEA 7:8–16 – 'Ephraim is a flat cake not turned over . . .
like a dove, easily deceived and senseless . . . They do not cry
to me from their hearts' (vv. 8,11,14, NIV).

Using vivid word pictures, the prophet Hosea condemned the
people's disloyalty to God to which the deterioration of their
national life bore eloquent witness. He said Israel was *half-baked*
(Jerusalem Bible), like a cake burnt to a coal at the bottom, with
raw dough at the top – an apt symbol of her stupid and sinful
inconsistencies. One writer has suggested that this figure includes
an indictment of the people for allowing the extremes of poverty
and wealth in their midst, and for the false separation they made
between sacred and secular – a show of worship on the Sabbath
and a go-as-you-please all the week.

Employing another colourful simile, the prophet said that Israel
was *like a dove, easily deceived and senseless*, flitting here and there,
uncertain where to place her political loyalty – now with Egypt,
then with Assyria (v. 11). In nations and in individuals, nothing
is more destructive of peace of mind, and more likely to alienate
the trust of others, than instability. We might ask ourselves: Can
we be relied upon?

There was, however, no greater indictment of the people than
when God said, 'They do not cry out to me from their hearts.' Not
only were the people inconsistent and unstable, they were *insincere*.
They said their prayers without really praying. Only prayers that
go from the heart reach God. But serving with words is never as
costly as serving with the heart. John Bunyan counselled: 'When
thou prayest, rather let thy heart be without words, than thy words
be without heart.'

SPOKESMEN FOR GOD

THE PAIN OF LOVE

HOSEA 11:7–11 – 'How can I give you up, Ephraim? How can I hand you over, Israel?' (v. 8, NIV).

In one of his books, Ian MacClaren tells the story of Lachlan Campbell, a good man and elder of the kirk, whose daughter Flora had left home lured by the bright lights of London. Lachlan heard of her shame and with trembling hand struck her name from the family Bible. But one day, wandering about the city, Flora drifted into a church and heard the preacher tell the story of the prodigal son. Her heart cried out, 'I will arise and go to *my* father.' She did and found that, as though he were the sinner, Lachlan confessed his terrible offence in erasing her name from the family Bible. Would she forgive him? But when Flora examined the Bible she found that her name had been scored out with wavering strokes, and that the ink had run as if it had been mingled with tears. As it had.

The wrongdoing of those we love always brings pain. This is what we see in the verse quoted above, which the eminent Old Testament scholar, George Adam Smith, described as 'the greatest passage in Hosea'. It is the heartcry of God, suffering over the sins of the people he loved, and is a foreshadowing of the Cross of Christ which Christians see not only as a demonstration of the sins of men, but also of the love and pain of God. Calvary echoes the cry, 'How can I give you up!' and shows the costliness of God's forgiveness of our sins.

THE CONSTANT APPEAL OF LOVE

HOSEA 14:1–3 – 'Return, O Israel, to the Lord your God . . .
take words with you and return to the Lord' (vv. 1,2, NIV).

It is thought by some Old Testament scholars that this final chapter
is not by Hosea. It would be strange, they say, if, after the final
pronouncement of doom in chapter 13, there should be this further
tender appeal to 'come back to the Lord'. Yet would it be so strange?
Is it not characteristic of the divine love to go on hoping that the
erring children might return home?

But even if these words of the final chapter are not by Hosea,
they breathe the spirit of his book. The prophet had no doubts
that despite the awful sins in which people become embroiled, the
love of God never lets them go. He gained this marvellous insight
through the bitter experience of his own broken marriage. The
whole Bible, and supremely the New Testament, bears witness to
the unwearying love of God.

Must we not confess that we have often stifled the voice of the
living God in our hearts as he has striven to lead us in his way;
that we have by our disobedience frequently thwarted and delayed
his will for us? Is it not true that we have rebelled against him
again and again? And we marvel at his patience! Despite our past
mistakes it is never too late to begin again.

> *O love that wilt not let me go,*
> *I rest my weary soul in thee;*
> *I give thee back the life I owe,*
> *That in thine ocean depths its flow*
> *May richer, fuller be.*
> *George Matheson*

REJECTION OF LOVE

ISAIAH 1:1–9 – 'I have reared children and brought them up, but they have rebelled against me' (v. 2, NIV).

We do not read of Isaiah's call until chapter 6, but the first chapter is important because it sets out God's case against Israel and is a fitting introduction to all that is to come. Following the first verse – an editor's introduction in which Isaiah and the times in which he lived are identified – God himself speaks. He reveals the depth of the tragedy of his sinful people – not only that they had broken his *law*, but that they had rebelled against his *love*. As Owen C. Whitehouse wrote, 'The sin of Israel . . . is not merely immoral; it is irreligious because it involves a personal relationship of antagonism to a divine will and a holy Fatherhood.'

Notice the moving emphasis on the word *they* in verse 2. God had 'brought them up' but they, *even they*, had rebelled against him. The sins of men always mean the sorrow of the Father-God.

The prophet himself points out the misery to which the people's rebellion had led (vv. 4–8) as he draws attention to some national calamity that had overtaken them – perhaps the Assyrian invasion of 701 BC. He sees that calamity as punishment. We, with our fuller knowledge of God's nature and grace, would hesitate to attribute such a happening to the direct action of God. Yet we must not deny the underlying principle here: sin always leads to misery, for when man sins he is rejecting the love of God he was made to enjoy.

Yet this reading ends on a note of hope. Despite man's many follies, God's love will never let him go.

'THINGS FALL APART'

ISAIAH 6:1–8 – 'In the year that King Uzziah died, I saw the Lord seated on a throne, high and exalted, and the train of his robe filled the temple' (v. 1, NIV).

The passing of King Uzziah may be compared with that of Queen Victoria in the sense that it ended a half-century of settled government, and therefore unsettled the people's minds. Uzziah had been a strong and successful ruler, but had become conceited and had performed temple sacrifices which should have been carried out only by the priests. He was then smitten with leprosy, which was interpreted as a punishment for his sins.

Isaiah was a courtier and perhaps a priest, since it was in the temple that he saw his vision and heard his call. It is significant that it was while the balance of his emotions was disturbed by the uncertainty created by the death of the only king he had known, that he saw his vision. God is not necessarily committed to maintaining the status quo. It is often in the unsettled times of life when 'things fall apart' that we see the truth and are most likely to respond to it.

As D.W. Cleverley Ford wrote in *A Theological Preacher's Notebook*: 'It was when that new opportunity opened up in your life that you came to believe in the goodness of the Lord. It was when your parents were taken from you . . . that you sought the sustaining hand of God in prayer. Deeper understanding of the Lord who reigns on high does not come through processes of abstract thought, it comes through the events intruding on our lives.'

Note, too, that having seen the need, Isaiah believed in 'do-it-yourself'! (v. 8).

NO PASSING THE BUCK

MICAH 1:1–9 – 'All this will happen because the people . . .
have sinned and rebelled against God. Who is to blame . . . ?
Samaria, the capital city itself! Who is guilty . . . ? Jerusalem
itself' (v. 5, GNB).

Today's reading is concerned with the judgment about to hit Judah.
('The Lord stands ready at Jerusalem's gate to punish her' – v. 9, LB).
Verse 5 makes it plain where the blame lay for the impending doom.
It lay with the people of Jerusalem themselves and their leaders, just
as the fall of Samaria (722 BC) could be put down to its people.
They could not make excuses and 'pass the buck', nor even blame
the invading Assyrians. They had asked for all that was coming
to them.

The American statesman, Daniel Webster, asked to say what was
the most important thought he had ever entertained, replied, 'My
individual responsibility to God.' The art of blame-shifting has been
perfected in our day, but the Christian can have no part of that.

Of course the blame lay *especially* with the national leaders. It
was in *Samaria* and *Jerusalem* that the canker proliferated. Yet
no man is an island unto himself. He is part of a community, a
body, and is either a healthy or a corrupting influence. Those in
the corridors of power, those who make policy, have the greater
responsibility for the community, but the Micahs, the peasants, are
not excused from concern for the body's health. And the Christian
does not opt out of public affairs.

Micah was not content to be a 'don't know', a 'floating voter' or
a non-voter. He realised the personal responsibility of his people,
his leaders, and himself for their communal plight, and sought to
do something about it.

THE HEART OF THE MATTER

MICAH 6:6–8 – 'God has told you what is good . . . Only to act justly, to love loyalty, to walk wisely before your God' (v. 8, NEB).

These verses – probably a fragment of a longer discourse – contain the heart of the Old Testament prophetic faith. The people ask a question in verses 6 and 7. How are they to approach God? Shall it be through the traditional apparatus of burnt-offerings and libations, culminating perhaps in the supreme sacrifice of a first-born son? This may date the passage to the reign of the reactionary King Manasseh (692–639) under whose rule these horrors were part of the establishment (2 Kings 21:6). They presuppose a God of fear and a time of anguish. Thus the Kingdom of Benin in West Africa attempted to ward off the British Expeditionary Force of 1894 with an orgy of human sacrifice, and won for their community the not entirely deserved title: 'City of Blood'.

Verse 8 shows, however, that even when Jerusalem was 'a city of blood', the underground prophetic movement kept up the great traditions of faith. God's requirements are simple: justice and 'mercy' (AV) or 'covenant love'. The idea includes both affection and loyalty. The RSV's 'steadfast love' attempts to convey both shades of meaning.

'This,' wrote George Adam Smith, 'is the greatest saying in the Old Testament.' But is it so easy to act justly and love loyalty? We admire Flora Macdonald, who protected Bonnie Prince Charlie in his wanderings . . . but are we made of the same metal? With fightings within and fears without, do we not crack under the strain? G.A. Smith saw a clue in one greater saying in the New Testament: 'Come unto me, all ye who labour and are heavy laden, and I will give you rest' (Matthew 11:28, AV).

CONVICTION AND DEPENDENCE

JEREMIAH 1:4–19 – 'The word of the Lord came to me, saying: "Before I formed you in the womb I knew you"' (v. 4, NIV).

Though utterly convinced of God's call, Jeremiah was reluctant to act upon it – a tension that remained with him throughout his life, yet one which brought him enrichment. The strong conviction and the hesitation were complementary, both essential to Jeremiah's discharge of the onerous task which God had assigned to him.

When the prophet's ministry later produced difficulties and even dangers, it was the conviction that God had placed his hand upon him that kept him at his post. With the certainty of a divine call, however, he also needed to retain his sense of dependence upon God, and discover through it the divine sufficiency; *self*-sufficiency would spell disaster.

Yet sensitive, tender Jeremiah never felt equal to his task and the consciousness of his inadequacy sent him to God again and again in an agony of self-pity and rebellion. In these encounters he learned a great deal about God, and here is found what John Skinner, in his great book *Prophecy and Religion*, calls 'the key to the significance of his personality as the first great exponent of individual and universal religion'.

The fact that there came a time in our lives when we could say truly, 'Now I belong to Christ', will always be our anchor in storm and stress. No less than Jeremiah we need such a conviction. But like Jeremiah we also need to retain our sense of dependence upon God. Woe to us when we become self-reliant. But as we *lean* on God, so we *learn* of him, and this is the source of the dynamic of our spiritual development.

FACING THE PROBLEM OF EVIL

JEREMIAH 12:5,6 – 'If you have raced with men on foot and they have worn you out, how can you compete with horses . . . how will you manage in the thickets of Jordan' (v. 5, NIV).

Here is the divine answer to Jeremiah's question about the prosperity of the wicked. Significantly it is a rebuke to his impatience and discouragement, somewhat akin to Jesus's words to Peter: 'What is that to you? You must follow me' (John 21:22). The prophet is reminded that a foot-weary soldier can hardly contend with cavalry, any more than a man when out of danger can face perils lurking in the jungles of Jordan: and this reflection brings Jeremiah the challenge – if present trials have caused such doubt of God, how can the more severe testing still to come be faced?

In answering the problem of evil, of which innocent suffering and unrighteous success are but two aspects, the Bible avoids philosophical speculation and calls upon the questioner to deepen his trust in God. For this is the only answer that matters: not rational explanation, but triumphant acceptance through implicit trust. Indeed, there is no other satisfactory answer, as distinct from attempted explanations, to life's bewildering experiences.

To surrender our faith through undeserved suffering probably indicates that, though we believe in God, we have believed the wrong things about him. *He* answers our problems, not by relieving us of them, but by being with us as *we* face them.

SPOKESMEN FOR GOD

IN THE HANDS OF THE POTTER

JEREMIAH 18:1–6 – 'The word of the Lord came to me: Can I not deal with you, Israel, says the Lord, as the potter deals with his clay?' (v. 6, NEB).

With his mind filled with thoughts of the future of Israel, Jeremiah watched the potter at work ... and suddenly he saw a vision of God's dealings with Israel. Israel was in God's hands as the clay was in the potter's, and the meaning of that truth was to be seen in the events which Jeremiah had just witnessed: 'Now and then a vessel he was making out of the clay would be spoilt in his hands, and he would start again and mould it into another vessel to his liking' (v. 4).

The picture, in the first instance, is of the sovereignty of God. People are not independent of the will of God, and they cannot live their lives in isolation from him. Ultimately people are in the hands of God and are subject to his eternal purposes.

But here is a further truth that the picture of the potter reveals: God's final purposes are not for destruction but for salvation and perfect wholeness. The spoiling of his immediate design does not mean complete rejection and uselessness; *God starts again*, and makes of the same clay another vessel that is pleasing to him.

The pangs of Creation
All suffered again –
O Artist-Creator
And Lover of men.
Kathleen Kendrick

125

COSTLY VISION

JEREMIAH 20:7–11 – 'But if I say, "I will not mention him or speak any more in his name," his word is in my heart like a burning fire, shut up in my bones' (v. 9, NIV).

First-hand experience of God results in deep conviction and strong inner compulsions. A man's enemies may persecute him, his friends entreat him, his own nature may cry out against the costliness of obedience, but he cannot deny his vision. Jeremiah was often torn between faithfulness to his mission and the shrinking of his own temperament. Derision is harder to endure than blows, and the average oriental hates ridicule.

Jeremiah had all this and more to contend with. But the word of the Lord, which brought him into such contempt, could not be contained. He must speak out whatever the cost.

William Penn, an early Quaker, was imprisoned in the Tower of London. The Quakers at that time were much misunderstood and hated. Particular objection was taken to their refusal to honour worldly rank, their pacifism and their refusal to swear on oath. William Penn was imprisoned because of his written defence of the Quakers. A message, supposedly from the Bishop of London, ordered him either to recant of what he had written or die a prisoner. Penn's reply was, 'My prison shall be my grave before I will budge a jot, for I owe my conscience to no mortal man.'

This strong but quiet certitude, the very opposite of fanaticism, is born of vital encounter with God. We cannot manufacture it at will. But we can remain open to God in a way which allows deep convictions like this to grow.

THE INWARDNESS OF TRUE RELIGION

JEREMIAH 31:31–34 – '"I will put my law in their minds and write it on their hearts. I will be their God and they will be my people"' (v. 33, NIV).

Early in Jeremiah's ministry the young and enthusiastic king of that time, Josiah, had instituted a series of reforms based on the covenant established at Sinai. The prophet appears to have supported these reforms at first, but as time went on he came to see that they could not really reach the heart of people's need, because they did not reach *the heart*. This was borne in upon him not only by observing what was happening around him on the social scene, but by an awareness of his own stubborn rebelliousness. He therefore placed emphasis on the inwardness of religion, 'that intimate fellowship of men with God from which truth, righteousness and love are the essential outflow' (John Mauchline).

The necessary thing in true religion is not the observance of external rules, but a change of nature. Rules have their place, particularly during spiritual immaturity (and who among us would claim to be mature?) but until goodness and right behaviour spring from within, they remain uncertain.

At the Last Supper Jesus recalled Jeremiah's prophecy when he said, 'This cup is the new covenant sealed by my blood' (1 Corinthians 11:25, NEB), claiming that the truth so astonishingly anticipated would be established by his own death. So Jesus prepared the way for the gospel, where we see that the essence of true religion is a personal relationship with God issuing in forgiveness of sins and a radical inner transformation. Is there any wonder that to describe this we use the term '*good* news'?

DOING OUR OWN WILL

JEREMIAH 42:1–18, 43:1–2 – 'When Jeremiah finished telling the people the words of the Lord their God . . . all the arrogant men said to Jeremiah, "You are lying!"' (vv. 1,2, NIV).

Jeremiah was among those who stayed behind in Jerusalem when a large number were taken into exile. Many of those who remained were making plans to go into Egypt away from war, domination by a cruel foreign power and the possibility of starvation in their devastated homeland. (Jeremiah himself was later taken there against his will.) But first they wanted to know the prophet's mind on the situation, and asked if he could help them. 'We swear we will do whatever the Lord your God sends you to tell us,' they said. 'Whether we like it not we will obey.'

After ten prayer-filled days Jeremiah went back to them to say that it was God's will that they remain in Jerusalem. In reply they 'had the effrontery' (NEB) to tell him he was lying.

It is easy for us all to accept only the advice we find agreeable. Indeed, too often we make our own plans, pray God's blessing on them and then deceive ourselves into thinking we are doing his will. It is much more difficult to ask God to guide as we make our plans and to be ready to adjust our own thinking at any point to conform to his.

Of course we cannot come before God with a completely blank mind; many factors must influence our thinking and colour our praying. But we should be aware of our prejudices. How tragic it is when self-centred desires make us deaf to God's voice and when we find 'good' reasons for evading the challenge of new directions!

SPOKESMEN FOR GOD

NO FAILURE

JEREMIAH 44:1–5,15–17 – ' "We will not listen to the message you have spoken to us in the name of the Lord!" ' (v. 16, NIV).

Not only did the people go down to Egypt in defiance of Jeremiah's words, they compelled the prophet to go with them. It is there we see the last of him, protesting vainly against the revival of idol worship among his countrymen. Tradition has it that he was stoned to death there.

From first to last, it appears, Jeremiah was a failure. No one listened to his message; he was regarded as a traitor; when he died, a reluctant exile, his country was in ruins and his people were scattered. Yet Jeremiah never gave up. He went on to the end working in God's name on behalf of the people who had rejected him.

Commenting on a book about Erasmus, the great sixteenth-century Christian, one writer said, 'He lived to see some of his followers burned to death by Catholics for being Protestants, and others beheaded by Protestants for being Catholics and himself despised or hated by both.' When he died the Pope placed all his writings on the forbidden index. 'But,' this commentator adds, 'Christians do not need reminding that to die an apparent failure . . . does not denote utter failure.'

To go on loving when love is not returned; to refuse to deny the truth however it is misrepresented; to hold to one's integrity whatever the cost . . . this makes for true success. 'Give me Christ crucified,' wrote Anthony Bridge, '. . . Give me Bonhoeffer who died in a Nazi jail for love of God . . .' – they appeared to fail, but they were in fact God's successes. And in the end it is only his assessment of any of us that really counts.

FULL CONFIDENCE

HABAKKUK 3:17–19 – 'I will rejoice in the Lord, I will be joyful in God my Saviour' (v. 18, NIV).

The last three verses of this prophecy move into an air of confidence which is deeply moving. It is also in sharp contrast to the questioning mood with which the book began. It certainly builds on the growing understanding of Habakkuk, and although all the outward evidences of God's providence are removed, he declares he will continue to rejoice in a Saviour-God. From the depth of despair Job made a similar response, 'Though he slay me, yet will I hope in him' (Job 13:15).

The whole of Christian history has been illuminated by people who had unshakeable confidence in God. The names of Stephen, Peter, Paul, Polycarp are well known from earliest times, and John and Betty Stam, Jim Elliott and the Inca martyrs are modern examples. Perhaps somewhat less well known is the story of Abdul Karim who was seized by a mob in Kabul, the capital of Afghanistan and given the choice of renouncing Christ or dying for his faith. He refused to recant and they cut off one of his arms. When he still persisted in his faith they cruelly removed the other arm. After that they sought again to persuade him to renounce Christ and when he refused they killed him.

Christian confidence in such circumstances stuns us, but also calls forth our admiration. Perhaps most of us have to ask ourselves whether we would be equal to such demands. Short of facing the actual circumstances we cannot know. However, what we can do is show our confidence in the God who saves by loyalty to the faith in our everyday experience.

AMENDMENT AND ACCEPTANCE

EZEKIEL 12:1–16 – 'Though they have eyes they will not see, though they have ears they will not hear, because they are a rebellious people' (v. 2, NEB).

The exiles in Babylon refused to believe that what had happened to them – that is, their deportation from Jerusalem – was going to happen to others, and that they would soon be joined in exile by fellow-countrymen deported from a devastated homeland. So Ezekiel resorted again to symbolic action, enacting the flight from Jerusalem that was about to take place. This is a remarkable prefiguring of the attempted escape of Zedekiah as described in 2 Kings 25:4.

The tragic element in the reading noted above – and it is seen again and again in the story of God's ancient people – is that they stubbornly resisted truth. Their spiritual faculties were so blunted that they were rapidly becoming incapable of recognising and responding to it, the more so because it was unpalatable to them.

It is never easy for any of us to face up to the unpleasant truth about ourselves, yet to do so is a sign of developing maturity. Certainly, until we do accept ourselves, 'warts and all', we are not going to do anything about our situation, or seek grace to help bring about the necessary amendment. There is much that can be effected in our own nature both by our conscious effort and also by the Spirit of God, but there are also parts of ourselves, and of our circumstances, which cannot be changed. Then the right thing to do is to come to terms with ourselves.

This means, as Ruth Fowke put it in her book, *Coping with Crises*, 'accepting our limitations as well as the exciting possibilities of our own particular nature.' And then, we may add, offering all we are to God. Here lies the way of peace.

VISION OF HOPE

EZEKIEL 37:1–14 – ' "Son of man, can these bones live? . . . Lord, you alone know" ' (v. 3, NIV).

The message of divine vindication, which Ezekiel had expressed earlier (chapter 36), is followed by this vision of hope. Jeremiah received such a message in the potter's workshop. Ezekiel hears God's word in an experience which has become the best known part of his prophecy.

It is important to remember that this is a vision, a very dramatic vision which has given rise to the popular spiritual, 'Dem bones, dem bones, dem dry bones'. Although that song makes us feel that the joints are clicking into place, we should not fail to 'hear the word of the Lord' which came to Ezekiel. The prophet, exiled in Babylon, is compelled to face the real issues of his situation. Can the nation ever rise from its humiliation? God's question echoes his own thought: 'Can these bones live?' (v. 3). The people themselves had already answered the question: 'They say, "Our bones are dried up and our hope is gone; we are cut off" ' (v. 11).

However, it is the vision that provides the proper answer, as verses 11 to 14 show. A resurrected and revitalised Israel would return to live in the land of promise. The message for the exiles is that they must not consider any situation hopeless, for God is in it with them, and can transform it according to his purpose.

That message remains valid. Our deliverance may be less dramatic than that envisaged by Ezekiel, but we have the confidence that God shares life's circumstances with us, and transforms us, whether our outward conditions are changed or not.

RIVER OF HEALING

EZEKIEL 47:1–12 – 'He said to me, "This water flows out to the region lying east, and down to the Arabah; at last it will reach the sea whose waters are foul, and they will be sweetened"' (v. 8, NEB).

In the later chapters of this book the prophet is concerned with plans for rebuilding the temple. Then he goes on to describe how, in another vision, he saw a stream of healing water flowing out from the temple, fertilising the desert places and making sweet waters of the Dead Sea. Ezekiel saw that the benefits of the worshipping community affect not only the worshippers but also spill over to the people round about.

How valuable true worship is to us! Worship means the response of the whole being to God. The NEB translation of Romans 12:1 goes: 'I implore you to offer your very selves to him: a living sacrifice, dedicated and fit for his acceptance, the *worship* offered by mind and heart.'

Such a response to God brings release and renewal to us, for true worship is 'one of the great healing and integrating influences in life'. But, alas, too many of us are obsessed with our own real and imagined needs when we come to the place of prayer, that what should be our first concern – the contemplation of the great and glorious God, as we see him in Jesus – is neglected. We are consequently the poorer. Only as we look upwards in worship will we find that healing of the spirit which is our great need.

Our worship also has value for others. Robert Newton Flew wrote that 'it is in our prayers that we draw on the resources of God for our work of helping others to him, and for the even greater task of transforming the common life of mankind.'

THE COMFORT OF GOD

ISAIAH 40:1–11 – 'Comfort, comfort my people, says your God. Speak tenderly to Jerusalem, and proclaim to her that her hard service has been completed, that her sin has been paid for' (vv. 1,2, NIV).

The Jews had been exiled in Babylon for forty years when the author of these chapters was called to the prophetic ministry. Although the captive Jews were more prosperous than their brethren who had been left behind in Jerusalem, they were spiritually dejected. It seemed that God had either forgotten or forsaken them.

What appeared to be divine indifference, however, was soon to end in God's dramatic intervention on their behalf. The prophet was to announce that national restoration was at hand. He visualised a great highway in the desert across which the captives would return to their homeland, led by God as sheep are led by the shepherd. God is never inactive in our lives: in this we can always take comfort. Deliverance, either out of distress, or in the midst of distress, is at hand for those who trust in him.

Long acquaintance with suffering and personal tragedy enabled Dick Sheppard to write to a fellow-sufferer: 'My friend, a letter is rather useless, but my deepest conviction is that love is the one thing to cling to in all the darkness. I am fifty-six years of age myself, and I too, in ways different from yours, have been disappointed and disillusioned a hundred times. But nothing and no one has been able to undermine my very simple faith that God is as Jesus Christ – though his love being so much greater than ours, may of necessity cause the painful process of disciplined suffering for his children.'

UNIMAGINABLE –
BUT NOT UNAPPROACHABLE

ISAIAH 40:27–31 – 'Those who hope in the Lord will renew their strength. They will soar on wings like eagles, they will run and not grow weary, they will walk and not faint' (v. 31, NIV).

Here is one of the delightful paradoxes of Scripture. The God who is beyond all human understanding, because we are too small and he is too great, is nevertheless the God who strengthens and renews those who trust in him. He is beyond our comprehension, but not beyond our apprehension. We may not grasp him by the intellect, but we may lay hold on him by faith.

The prophet Jeremiah had stressed the tender condescension of God, whilst Ezekiel had later emphasised the transcendent character of the divine. This prophet wonderfully combines both truths, for they are equally important. Religion frequently fails to achieve this balance with the result that we make God either too remote, or too trivial.

True trust in God is independent of favourable circumstances. When the prophet commenced his ministry the situation in which the Jews found themselves seemed a total denial of God's providence. But 'true religion is a conviction of the character of God, and a resting upon that alone for salvation,' wrote George Adam Smith. The man who has this conviction can be, as Victor Hugo said, like the bird who sings on unafraid when the bough on which she has rested sways beneath her, for she knows she has wings. Relying unconditionally on the character of God gives us both the eagle wings of vision and stamina for the long trudge; it inspires ecstasy and endurance; it is the secret of enthusiasm and patience.

THE GREATNESS OF PROPHECY

ISAIAH 61:1–3 – 'The Spirit of the Sovereign Lord is on me, because the Lord has anointed me to preach good news to the poor. He has sent me to bind up the broken-hearted, to proclaim freedom for the captives and release for the prisoners' (v. 1, NIV).

To the Israelites struggling with their adverse circumstances these words were welcomed with their promise of better days to come. Had the prophet known that one day the Messiah himself would publicly take the scroll and read these magnificent words, applying them to himself, he would have been overwhelmed. They were inspired words, bearing the authority of the Spirit of God, by whom all true prophets were anointed.

Israel's kings were anointed with oil, as were the High Priests, but the Messiah – the very name means 'anointed one' – was anointed by the Spirit. The Spirit of God indwelt the Messiah, empowering him to bring deliverance to God's people and to establish his kingdom.

When Jesus confronted with his true identity the congregation in Nazareth, to whom he was known from boyhood (Luke 4:22), he had behind him his unique birth, the experience of the baptism of water by John the Baptist, and the descent of the Spirit from Heaven. He had also, under the direction of the Spirit, experienced the temptations in the wilderness. He was ready to resume his role of Messiah.

Part of the greatness of prophecy is that it so often speaks in a way greater than the prophet had either intended or could even imagine. Isaiah spoke of larger issues than he knew. Let us ponder the accurate way in which the Scripture's truths speak to us today, helping us to understand God's will. The words carry a tremendous relevance for us.

WHEN WE DOUBT GOD'S LOVE

MALACHI 1:1–5 – ' "I have loved you," says the Lord. But you ask, "How have you loved us?" ' (v. 2, NIV).

The disillusionment of the Israelites following their return from exile was reflected in the scant concern they were giving, in Malachi's time, to religion and morality. Though the temple at Jerusalem had been restored, there was little evidence of the prosperity the people had been led to expect by the prophets Second Isaiah, Haggai and Zechariah. Their cry, 'How have you loved us?' expressed their conviction that God had let them down.

Malachi's reply to their question was hardly satisfactory. Of what comfort was it to know that, if they felt themselves badly done to, Esau (ie the Edomites, a neighbouring people) was worse off? And obviously, the prophet's answer lacked the deeper insight that God's love applies to Edom as well as to Israel. Yet, despite their limitations, the first few verses of this little book remind us of the eternal truth, so clearly shown in Jesus, that even when events and circumstances seem to deny it, God is love.

Not all doubting people ask, 'Where is the evidence for God?' There are many who are convinced about his existence but who nevertheless doubt his benevolence. Their question is, 'Where is the evidence for *the love of God*?' The Christian gospel asserts that Jesus is both the proof and the measure of God's generosity.

Part 6

THE ONWARD MARCH
OF THE GOSPEL

The title J.B. Phillips gave to his translation of the Acts of the Apostles, *The Young Church in Action*, is most apt. What that title says: that it was a *young* church, and that it was a *busy*, active church should be fully appreciated.

The Acts is Luke's second volume of his account of the origins and progress of Christianity. The first, his Gospel, takes us up to the Ascension of Jesus. The second continues from there and takes us, with Paul the prisoner, to Rome. So, firstly, we travel, as it were, from Bethlehem and Nazareth to Jerusalem, the central city of *the Jews*; then we travel from Jerusalem to Rome, the central city of *the world*.

Luke makes a vivid record of remarkable events, and as we read we can't fail to be carried along by the energy and excitement of it all.

At the beginning, centre-stage, humanly speaking, is Peter. (Of course, truly at centre-stage is the Holy Spirit – it all began when he came upon those first followers.) At chapter seven (with one brief mention) and then at chapter nine, Saul – later Paul – comes into the picture. We are going to hear a lot more of him. Then we are back with Peter, making his significant contribution; but at chapter thirteen we are back again with Paul – still called Saul – and he remains at the centre for the rest of the story.

Luke – a Gentile himself – is showing how the Gentiles entered into the Church on an equal footing with the Jews, that Christianity is a world-embracing religion. The difficulties over, and setbacks to, this revolutionary idea are faithfully recorded. The meeting held in Jerusalem to settle the Gentiles-in-the-church question, and recorded in chapter fifteen, was crucial. Peter's eloquent speech (vv. 7–11), and the witness of Paul and Barnabas to their own reception in the Gentile world, opened the way for the preaching of a universal gospel.

That had to happen or the Church would have remained a sect within Judaism, and God's plan from the beginning, when he said to Abraham that 'all peoples on earth will be blessed through you' (Genesis 12:3, NIV), would, humanly speaking, have been frustrated.

But the Holy Spirit prevailed – and the comments that follow show something of the wonder of that.

WIND AND FIRE

ACTS 2:1–13 – 'All of them were filled with the Holy Spirit and began to speak in other tongues as the Spirit enabled them' (v. 4, NIV).

Although this passage contains some puzzling details, its importance in relation to everything that follows cannot be exaggerated. It occupies the same crucial position in the story of the Church as does the account of the Spirit's descent upon Christ at his baptism in the Gospel narrative.

As Greek was spoken throughout the ancient world it was certainly not *necessary* for the disciples to speak in other languages. Were they, as has been suggested, astonishingly freed from the limitations and peculiarities of dialect? Or was this the gift of ecstatic speech such as Paul mentions in his letter to the Corinthian Church (12:27f.)? It may be best to interpret all the outward signs of the Spirit's coming – the tongues, wind and fire – in terms of popular belief that such phenomena would mark the coming of the Messianic age.

Wind and fire are great elemental symbols which transcend any interpretation we may give to them. The wind of the Spirit has never ceased to blow. Sometimes it is a 'gentle zephyr, sometimes a judgment hurricane, sometimes a quiet guiding voice in the hour of meditation, sometimes a fierce tornado casting down the strongholds of the powers of darkness in the name of Christ – always the Spirit of God is at work' (James Stewart). We have no longer to pray for the coming of the Spirit, but rather to seek to discern his presence and be fully open to his influence.

HEALING MINISTRY

ACTS 3:1–10 – ' "I have no silver or gold; but what I have I give you: in the name of Jesus Christ of Nazareth, walk" ' (v. 6, NEB).

Christ commanded his disciples to preach the gospel *and heal the sick*. When Peter and John saw the lame man being carried to his daily begging site they obeyed Christ's command and used the authority he had invested in them. One thing at least is clear from this: God wills health for the whole person – body, mind and spirit.

What is sometimes called 'spiritual healing' has never entirely died out in the Church, although it is obvious that healing now comes largely through modern medicine. Is it any less of God? Most Christians now see the Church's obedience to Christ's command in terms of the fullest co-operation with all agencies seeking people's wholeness. At the same time the Church has a particular ministry of prayer, faith and declaration of God's pardon.

Many Christian sufferers feel led to a position similar to that of Audrey Shepherd, who contracted polio at the age of thirty. 'For me,' she writes, 'disability means learning to live a double life! At the same time as accepting my present limitations and seeking to take a new place in the community, I must work with God for wholeness, and that is done secretly in the heart.'

Acceptance and co-operation for wholeness: this is a somewhat paradoxical attitude, but it is the only one which reflects both the truth that God wills our healing and the fact that suffering is deeply mysterious and must sometimes be transcended rather than removed.

FAITH AND FREEDOM

ACTS 3:11–26 – 'The name of Jesus, by awakening faith, has strengthened this man' (v. 16, NEB).

Peter's message to the crowd which gathered in Solomon's Porch was typical of the early preaching. It interpreted God's action and called for the people's response. In this case the act of God was the healing of the lame man. But Peter immediately linked this with the divine revelation in Jesus Christ. It is particularly significant that the apostle acquits the people of Jerusalem, and even their rulers, of deliberate wickedness. Could this view have any other basis than the prayer of Jesus from the Cross, 'Father forgive them; for they know not what they do'?

Peter explained the healing of the man by saying that the name of Jesus had awakened faith. At least, this is the New English Bible rendering of the very confused Greek of the original text. In the New Testament, people not only have faith *in* Jesus, they are led into faith *by* Jesus. He is the pioneer of faith.

In his book *The Free Man* Ronald Gregor Smith wrote of some of the misconceptions about faith. Faith is not something which requires a special talent or taste 'similar to a liking for caviare or an appreciation of the music of Stravinsky', nor is it a burden added to ethical demands laid upon the Christian, 'the last straw that breaks the camel's back'. Faith is our free response to the forgiving word of God addressed to us in Christ. There is no burden here, only a liberation.

WE CAN'T DO EVERYTHING

ACTS 6:1–7 – ' "We should spend our time preaching, not administering a feeding programme," [the Twelve] said ... "Select seven men, wise and full of the Holy Spirit ... and we will put them in charge of this business" ' (vv. 2,3, LB).

Even in a community as close to Pentecost as this, one in which materialism was to be banished by communal ownership, it was not long before there was a dispute. Not that there was necessarily any dishonesty or improper motive, but even when the principle of fair shares is accepted by all there may be inefficiency in distribution and therefore injustice. Unfortunately, as so often happens, it was a racial minority that was neglected.

So the apostles came up against a problem that often recurs in the Christian ministry. If the minister accepts the social implications of the gospel and tries to meet all the social needs he sees, this aspect of his work mushrooms by a religious Parkinson's law until his spiritual functions are almost totally eclipsed. If he is effectively to fulfil his vocation he must find a way of hiving off some of the responsibility for social work. This was no new problem. Jesus often told people to keep quiet about his healing powers, so that he would not have to spend all his time on his healing ministry.

The important thing to notice is that though seven deacons were to exercise a different ministry it was not subsidiary to preaching but complementary to it, and no less wisdom and godliness were required. G.T. Stokes says of it, 'It was a life-long office, in the exercise of which maturity of judgment, of piety and of character were required.' Whatever our work in the Church, Christlikeness is the first requirement.

HALF A TRUTH IS WORSE THAN NONE!

ACTS 6:8–15 – ' "This man," they said, "is always talking against our sacred Temple and the Law of Moses. We heard him say that this Jesus of Nazareth will tear down the Temple and will change all the customs that have come down to us from Moses" ' (vv. 13,14, GNB).

It is rather surprising that all seven deacons had Greek names rather than Hebrew, and that one, Nicolas, was 'a Gentile . . . who had earlier been converted to Judaism' (v. 5). This was no doubt because the apostles were falling over backwards to meet the complaints of the Greek-speaking Christians (v. 1). But it also suggests that the Christian Church was allowing Gentiles more influence than some non-Christian Jews would be prepared to accept.

Their reaction is an indication that a worldly man's action is more often determined by emotion rather than by logic or truth. They began by 'arguing with Stephen' (v. 9), but found that the Holy Spirit enabled him to refute their arguments (v. 10). They did not surrender their viewpoint, however, but resorted to bribery and false witness (v. 11).

Having lost the argument, therefore, Stephen's opponents distort the truth. As is so often the case, they do not assert what is clearly untrue, but employ a half-truth which has enough truth in it to convince the unthinking and enough error to destroy the cause of truth. Jesus *had* spoken figuratively about his body as a Temple to be destroyed and resurrected in three days (John 2:19–21), and *had* shown the inadequacies of the Law (Matthew 5:17–48). His purpose, however, was not destructive but transforming. Half a truth is often more damaging of truth than falsehood.

THE BLOOD OF THE MARTYRS

ACTS 7:54–60 – 'Stephen, filled through all his being with the Holy Spirit, looked steadily up to heaven . . . "Look!" he exclaimed, "the heavens are opened and I can see the Son of Man standing at God's right hand!"' (vv. 55,56, JBP).

The Christian's duty is sometimes to raise his voice in protest even if this has no practical effect. It is also sometimes his duty to do so even if it costs him dear, as we see here in the lynching of Stephen. It was when Stephen saw most clearly, and was most convinced of, the Christian gospel (that Jesus was the Son of Man, God's right hand man), that the people attacked him, for they were so far from the truth which Stephen spoke that they thought it blasphemy. In their view God reigned alone and the thought that Jesus was sharing his power and glory 'touched them on the raw' (v. 54, NEB).

We need not interpret Stephen's vision in too physical a sense. G.T. Stokes writes, 'Stephen did not need a keen vision and an open space and a clear sky, free from clouds and smoke . . . Had [he] been in a dungeon and his eyes been blind, the spiritual vision might still have been granted.' His vision, however, made him triumphant. 'He saw the martyr's death as the gateway to the throne of Christ' (William Barclay).

He unhesitatingly committed his eternal spirit to the Lord Jesus (v. 59) just as the Lord Jesus had committed his to God the Father. He forgave those who were the instruments and instigators of his death (v. 60) as Jesus had also done. And if we go to verse 1 of the next chapter we find, as Augustine said, that 'The Church owes Paul to the prayer of Stephen.'

GOSPEL OF CONVERSION

ACTS 9:1–9 – 'Suddenly a light flashed from the sky all around him. He fell to the ground and heard a voice saying, "Saul, Saul, why do you persecute me?"' (vv. 3,4, NEB).

The amazing character of Paul's conversion is recognised when the intensity of his persecution of the Christians is considered. Luke says that 'Saul harassed the Church bitterly' (Acts 8:3, JBP), employing a verb that is used of 'mangling or mauling by wild animals' (G.W.H. Lampe). Saul's measures were relentless and thorough. He believed the Christians were wrong and as a proud Jew felt he must fight unceasingly to destroy the false faith. But he encountered Christ on the Damascus road and from that moment became his loving and obedient follower.

The gospel is concerned with the conversion of people, though every person's experience of conversion is not as sudden and colourful as Paul's. People discover Christ, and have their lives set on his Kingdom, in quite different ways. But of the reality and necessity of conversion, however it comes, no Christian should be in any doubt.

In a letter to a Salvation Army publication in 1878, a writer described the effects of the changed ways of some miners after their conversion: 'Instead of drunkenness, oaths and all kinds of sin, the voice of praise and thanksgiving is everywhere heard. In one colliery the very horses can't make out what has happened, the treatment they receive is so very different from that to which they have been accustomed!'

The effects of other conversions, like the experience itself, may be less dramatic. Some may simply say that since their conversion (in the words of a hymn) 'Heaven above is softer blue, earth around is sweeter green . . .' But both types of conversion may express a real inner experience.

ACCEPTING OTHERS

ACTS 9:10–19 – 'So Ananias went. He entered the house, laid his hands on him and said, "Saul, my brother"' (v. 17, NEB).

From the Damascus road, the scene of Paul's conversion, the story transfers to Damascus itself, to a disciple there named Ananias. We can readily understand this man's doubts about receiving Saul, for he was well-known as an enemy of the faith. But it is a mark of Ananias's obedience to God – an essential characteristic of Christian discipleship – that notwithstanding his doubts, he did exactly what God asked of him. When he met Saul he called him 'my brother', and showed how truly he had caught the spirit of Jesus, which is the spirit of forgiving acceptance.

We may learn from this incident how necessary it is for all of us as Christians to accept people as persons, something we can do with success only in so far as we know ourselves to have been accepted by God. Even then it does not come easily to everyone to accept others. Not everyone is naturally good at human relationships; nevertheless Christians of all people should make sincere efforts in this direction. It certainly was not easy for Ananias, as his own words show.

Writing on this point, Mark Gibbard suggested that we may learn a good deal about accepting people by watching and reading about others with a gift for this. He mentions Forbes Robinson, living as a chaplain of a Cambridge college. 'To him not one was a "mere student, one of a mass"; he made the most ordinary person feel for himself that "his own life, however commonplace, with all its failures and inconsistencies, was a tremendous enterprise, big with opportunities"' (*Why Pray?*). Perhaps we should make a resolve to help others in this way.

UNIVERSALITY AND OPENNESS

ACTS 13:1–3 – 'The Holy Spirit said, "Set Barnabas and Saul apart for me, to do the work to which I have called them." Then . . . they . . . let them go' (vv. 2,3, NEB).

Following his conversion and a subsequent visit to Jerusalem, Saul went on to his home town, Tarsus. After recording this (Acts 9:28–30) the narrator, Luke, focuses on other events in which Saul did not figure, an indication that, however fascinating a figure Saul was, what really mattered was not what *he* was doing but how the work of God was proceeding. We next read of Saul when it is recorded (11:25) that he was brought by Barnabas from Tarsus to Antioch. There he lived – save for a short visit to Jerusalem, 11:27–36 – until he undertook his missionary work, of which this reading marks the beginning.

There are two observations to be made about these three verses. They show that the first believers were drawn from a variety of backgrounds and places. Simeon may have been a negro, Lucian hailed from Cyrene in North Africa, Manaen had moved in royal circles and Saul and Barnabas were from Tarsus and Cyprus respectively.

This brings a reminder of the universality of Christianity, and the allied thought that no denomination has a monopoly of truth. In his book, *The Truth about the Early Church*, William Neil pointed out, 'No branch of the Church can claim to reproduce in its present practice or structure the Church that Luke describes in Acts.'

This reading also points to the necessity for Christians to be always open to God. God spoke, and the believers at Antioch heard and obeyed. Someone has said, however, that 'It is not always that we cannot hear God speaking; it is sometimes that we do not want to hear' – and that is a challenging thought for us all!

LIBERATING GOSPEL

ACTS 13:4–12 – 'Instantly mist and darkness came over him
and he groped about for someone to lead him by the hand'
(v. 11, NEB).

Was Paul's treatment of Elymas the sorcerer out of harmony with
the Spirit of Jesus, who refused to call down fire from heaven on
those who opposed *him*? In his book, *The Acts of the Apostles, A
Study in Interpretation*, C.J. Barker suggests that Paul acted under
'an overwhelming impulse which was taken (by the narrator) to
come from the Holy Spirit'. This commentator wonders whether
Sergius Paulus, therefore, was only dazzled by a miracle, and
suggests that on this occasion Paul had not perhaps won a real
victory for Christ.

If this is accepted we may learn from the incident that even a man
like Paul was subject to errors of judgment, and we need not then
be surprised at the mistakes of lesser men. And we may take heart
when recollection of our own mismanaging of situations causes us
to despair that we will ever be able to please God in our personal
relationships.

Perhaps the sorcerer's blindness (which was only temporary) was
caused by his own intense emotional reaction as the truth declared by
Paul's message showed the falsity of his own teaching. The blindness
of Elymas has been likened to the blindness of Paul on the Damascus
road. The Venerable Bede wrote, 'The apostle, remembering his own
example, knew that from the darkness of the eye the mind's darkness
might be restored.' It was so with Paul, but we do not know whether
it was so with Elymas.

We may say this with certainty, however: the Christian gospel,
with its clear declaration of the divine love which makes people
whole, is very different from occultism, fortune-telling and magic.
These bring misery, fear and despair: the gospel always brings
liberty, hope and joy.

GOD IN HISTORY

ACTS 13:13–16,32–43 – 'God has brought to Israel the Saviour Jesus, as he promised' (v. 23, NIV).

One probable reason why John Mark returned to Jerusalem was that he resented Paul's growing ascendancy over his uncle, Barnabas. At the beginning of the journey we read of 'Barnabas and Saul'; from this point the missionaries are referred to as 'Paul and his companions' and, later, 'Paul and Barnabas'. The eventual outcome of John Mark's desertion was that later when Paul wished to embark on a second journey he and Barnabas split up over the question of John Mark accompanying them again. So two journeys were undertaken, one led by Paul and the other by Barnabas. This may be seen as an illustration of how God can take people's mistakes and weaknesses and turn them into good.

If possible the whole of Paul's sermon at Antioch should be read for it shows the pattern of the first Christian preaching, in which Jesus is seen as the culmination of God's great acts in history, of which the Old Testament is the record.

Paul's sermon would have particular point and challenge for the predominantly Jewish congregation, but it is still significant. The Old Testament story is a necessary part of our Christian Scriptures and essential reading for us today. This is because, as Paul so eloquently declared, what commenced with Abraham and continued in the nation of which he was the 'father', reached at last to him who is the Saviour of the world.

Paul demonstrated the relevance of Jesus with both sound argument and passion. We, however – who share his responsibility to make Jesus known – may not have the gift of eloquence. Then let us remember that the most effective medium for declaring the gospel is never our words, but the way we live our lives.

RESOLVING THE DISPUTE

ACTS 15:1–11 – 'The apostles and elders met to consider this question' (v. 6, NIV).

The question of Gentile admission to the household of faith was of fundamental importance. The issue was basic to the well-being and even the existence of the Church. Unless the problems were ventilated and thoroughly discussed and decided, there was a grave danger of division between the churches of Jerusalem and Judaea on the one hand, and the church of Antioch and its daughter-churches on the other. To resolve the matter the Church called a meeting.

The simple fact we observe here is that there was no magical formula for solving the problem, no mystical vision that immediately provided the answer. Certainly the Spirit of God was at work (v. 8), but he was working through the human instruments that were his. So the Church took the commonsense and practical step of bringing the believers together, and through their discussions and their testimony to the Spirit's working, the will of God became clear.

Writing about his relationship with William Booth in the early days of The Salvation Army, his son Bramwell, his 'chief executive officer', spoke of his father's patience in hearing 'all that we had to say against what he thought best', and of William's evident desire 'to do what was for the highest welfare of the Army and the Kingdom of God'. And Bramwell added, 'He was very agreeable to do business with. Conferences were a reality. No time was begrudged, no labour spared, to explore fully the questions before him.'

In such ways moves the Spirit of God.

GOD'S DECISION

ACTS 15:12–21 – 'Simon has described to us how God at first showed his concern by taking from the Gentiles a people for himself' (v. 14, NIV).

Peter's contribution to the Jerusalem Council seems to have marked a turning point in the proceedings. One writer has said, 'It is Peter that we must credit for lifting the discussion out of the realm of opinion – an acrimonious and fruitless discussion of law and precedent – on to the high plane of God's authority.'

Referring to the conversion of Cornelius (cf. Acts 10), Peter emphasised that it was God who had directed that the gospel should be taken to the Gentiles, and he confirmed what had been done by giving them his Holy Spirit. Peter's message to the council was straightforward and powerful: Whom God had accepted they had not to reject.

With that the matter was virtually decided. The people who had been debating fiercely were silenced (v. 12). It remained but for Paul and Barnabas to confirm the point from their own experience, and then James summed up the debate . . . and reminded the believers that Scripture all along had spoken of that very thing.

When confronted by uncertainties on the Christian way it is not always required that we seek some new revelation of God's will for us. Sometimes the answer lies within our past experience: what God the Holy Spirit has already been doing within us and through us may be the indication of his will for us in the future. Perhaps his decision for us has already been made. It needs our acknowledgment and response. Our prayer should be: 'Lord, help us to see what you are already doing, and to follow where you are leading.'

DIVINE LEADING

ACTS 16:6–10 – 'After Paul had seen the vision, we got ready at once to leave for Macedonia, concluding that God had called us to preach the gospel to them' (v. 10, NIV).

'Maintaining spiritual contact with God,' wrote William Temple, 'produces, it would seem, a sensitiveness to the Divine Will which usually shows itself only in the actions which it prompts . . . I have found that at times when I have been taking due trouble about my devotional life I have frequently felt an unreasoned impulse to see someone whom (as it turned out) I was able to help considerably. I have also noticed that if I get slack about my prayers, such coincidences cease.'

Such experiences of the guidance of God were also known by Paul, as we find in this reading. For a time there was uncertainty as to the way the evangelistic band should go. First they were prevented from going further west into Asia Minor (v. 6) and then they thought of going north-east into Bithynia, but found themselves unable to do so (v. 7ff.). Finally they came to Troas, and in a vision one night Paul saw clearly what they had to do – they had to cross over into Macedonia. Looking on the event now, we can see it was the beginning of the evangelisation of Europe and the Western world. It was a giant step forward.

As our reading clearly testifies, such 'inspiration' is the work of God's Holy Spirit. He illumines our minds and opens our eyes. Times of uncertainty may be simply his closing the door on certain fields of service, that we shall be brought to the place where we can receive his guidance for the future.

BEARING INDIFFERENCE

ACTS 17:16–23 – 'All the Athenians and the foreigners who lived there spent their time doing nothing but talking about and listening to the latest ideas' (v. 21, NIV).

Athens had once been the stimulating, intellectual centre of all that was best in Greek science and art. In Paul's day, however, it was but a shadow of its former self, living on past glories and showing little evidence of real enquiry after truth.

This is indicated in Luke's indictment of the Athenians (v. 21 above; cf. 17:32ff.). They were, he said, only concerned with talking about the latest novelty. They loved discussions and debates, but not so that it would demand a response from them or have any effect on their lives. They gave a place to God in their philosophical systems – and Athens was not devoid of altars – but again this acknowledgement made no practical difference to their way of living.

The situation facing Paul as he rose to address the Court of Areopagus was that of an ultimately shallow intellectualism, which tacitly held to belief in God yet regarded itself superior to all religion, and which felt free and able to examine all claims while committing itself to nothing.

Surely the hardest audience Paul ever had to face was not one of those where he was denounced and persecuted, but this one where men showed in the end that they simply did not care – about him or his message. The experience, it seems, shook Paul as nothing else did, and drove him back to Christ crucified (cf. 1 Corinthians 2:2ff.), who also had been laughed at and rejected and dismissed. But in Christ, we may believe, Paul found the strength to continue.

THE POWER OF TRUTH

ACTS 19:23–41 – 'There is danger not only that our trade will lose its good name, but also that the temple of the great goddess Artemis will be discredited' (v. 27, NIV).

The making and selling of silver shrines of the goddess Diana, who was worshipped under several titles throughout Asia Minor, was a flourishing trade in Ephesus. There was also in the city a temple dedicated to the goddess which was one of the seven wonders of the world and doubtless a tourist attraction. That the trade was affected to the extent that Demetrius felt he had to do something about the situation was proof of the success of Paul's preaching, but more so of the power of the gospel to revolutionise people's lives.

People are greatly mistaken who think that Christianity always supports the established order, though sadly enough it has often been the case. The gospel is not committed to any earthly scheme of things: it is committed only to truth. What happened at Ephesus when Paul preached the gospel was that the truth upset the established way – and this has happened again and again in the history of the Church. It has consequently sometimes brought suffering to the believers, like, for example, those early-day Salvationists who were attacked in their open-air meetings by unruly mobs hired by publicans whose trade was suffering because so many converts were being made.

It is an indictment of us when our desire for peace and comfort is stronger than our desire for truth. But in the long run it is only the truth that will minister to our best and highest interests for, as Jesus said, it is only by the truth that we can be set free.

AGONISING CHOICE

ACTS 21:17–26 – 'When he had greeted them he gave them a detailed account of all that God had done among the Gentiles through his ministry, and they, on hearing this account, glorified God' (vv. 19,20, JBP).

Paul's arrival in Jerusalem, bringing the Gentile churches' collection for impoverished Jewish believers, was both welcomed and feared by the local Christian leaders. Grateful as they were to hear of the gospel's triumphs among the Gentiles, they were also under considerable pressure from conservative Jews who viewed Paul with grave suspicion. To disarm criticism and to prove his continued support for the Law as far as Jews were concerned, it was suggested that Paul should pay the expenses of four men who were under a vow. With what misgivings the writer of the letter to the Galatians complied we can only imagine!

Reflected in this incident we see those instances when we are compelled to agonise between equally unattractive alternatives. In a study of concentration camp survivors Wilfred Noyce maintains that this was a constant dilemma. A 'certain minimum lowering of standards' was essential, for instance, in being willing to fight for one's portion of food. Yet the slippery slope of compromise led to disintegration. One survivor suggested it was helpful to draw a line at the outset: 'Thus far I will go but no farther, or the life which I preserve will have lost its value.'

No 'rule of thumb' can be devised for every moral dilemma. When each course of action is un-ideal three possessions will prove invaluable: insight into our own motives; a love for people greater than our desire for tidy solutions; and the resolve not to surrender vital principles.

LIKE MASTER – LIKE SERVANT

ACTS 21:33–40 – 'The whole mass of the people followed, shouting, "Away with him!"' (v. 36, JM).

Fortunately for Paul, the Tower of Antonio was close by the temple so that Roman soldiers from there came swiftly to his rescue. That the infuriated crowd echoed the cry 'Away with him!', which arose twenty-five years earlier at the trial of Jesus, would not surprise Paul who never doubted that the disciple should share his Lord's sufferings.

In Albert Camus' story *The Stranger*, a young man charged with motiveless murder appeared before a magistrate. Vainly the older man tried to understand the prisoner. 'But why, why did you go on firing at a prostrate man?' he asked. The accused remained silent. Suddenly the magistrate arose, walked to a filing cabinet standing against the opposite wall and took from it a silver crucifix, which he waved as he came back to the desk. Despite repeated attempts to penetrate the young man's indifference with the assurance that 'even the worst of sinners could obtain forgiveness of [Christ]', the magistrate obtained no response.

Was Camus hinting at one reason for the Church's failure? asks Geoffrey Ainger. Did he mean us to recognise in the figure of the pious magistrate 'waving' the cross a Church improperly related to its Lord? 'Jesus did not call us to wave the cross. He called us to carry it!' Paul did precisely that, as must all true messengers of the cross.

DIVINE OVERRULING

ACTS 25:1–12 – '"You have appealed to Caesar. To Caesar you will go"' (v. 12, NIV).

Paul's appeal to Caesar, and the journey to Rome that followed as a consequence perfectly illustrates the twin-truths that God can use even human evil as an instrument of his will, and that his ultimate purpose can never know defeat.

To visit Rome was Paul's great ambition, which God had assured him should be realised (23:11). Yet no promise could ever have seemed less likely of fulfilment in view of all that had happened since it was given – the trial before Felix and that man's unwillingness to reach a decision, the two-year wait in prison, and then the change in the governorship of the province. Yet now the way was open, and though Paul was to make the journey as a prisoner, he would be enabled, as God had said, to bear witness to Christ there.

In the ultimate the will of God always prevails. It may happen in ways other than those we envisage, and there may be delays according to our time-bound thinking; but God's purpose can never know defeat. We may apply this truth to our prayers. God never ignores our prayers even though we might sometimes be tempted to think he does. Sometimes his answer may have to be delayed because we are not ready for it. Sometimes we may have to be given time to see that the request was immature and unwise anyway, and that we should therefore substitute another prayer or abandon it altogether as unworthy and impossible of fulfilment – in our own highest interests.

And there lies the heart of the matter. God is concerned with our true welfare, and in one way or another he will see that this is achieved – a wonderfully comforting thought.

THE ONE ESSENTIAL

ACTS 26:1–18 – ' "I saw a light from heaven . . . and I heard a voice saying to me in Aramaic, 'Saul, Saul, why do you persecute me?' " ' (vv. 13,14, NIV).

Because Paul had exercised his right of appeal to Rome, Festus had to find some explanation for sending him there. As yet he did not have one. So he was thankful when King Agrippa paid him a courtesy call, thinking that if he brought Paul before *him*, something might emerge which would provide the explanation he required. So a meeting was arranged and there, as always, the apostle grasped the opportunity to speak for Christ.

If there was one thing of which Paul was sure, it was that his faith in Christ was not misplaced. During the Second World War a young German soldier stationed in Russia wrote to a Christian minister, Helmut Thielicke: 'How quickly now it can be all over for me. This is why I would like to be clear about what may be relied upon to the end. Is it Christ? He is an ideal for me . . . but can I build my life on him? Is he still only one among many who have walked this earth before me, even if he is the greatest. But I have to be able to believe that he is the Son of God if he is to be my Saviour. And the trouble is right there; at that point I am quite helpless.' Paul could never have written like that. Of Christ his Saviour he *was* sure.

There are things of which we Christians may sometimes be uncertain, but to be sure of Christ is the one essential. The person who can say, 'I know whom I have believed', has a faith no one can destroy. As Herbert Butterfield famously said, 'Hold to Christ, and for the rest be totally uncommitted'.

THE BEST OF WORDS OF LIFE

PERILOUS JOURNEY

ACTS 27:1–8 – 'Julius, in kindness to Paul, allowed him to go to his friends so they might provide for his needs' (v. 3, NIV).

Everything seemed to be against Paul. He was only making the journey at all because his appeal meant Festus had to send him to Caesar when otherwise he might have been freed (26:32). The winds were against him, not only as they skirted round Cyprus, which they might expect, but also when they changed vessels and carried on from Myra in an Alexandrian grain ship (27:38). The delays were so late that winter came upon them, when sensible sailors put to shore and sheltered for three months.

Yet Paul was not alone on his journey to Rome. Luke was with him, for he starts again to say 'we' did this, and 'we' did that, rather than 'they' did such and such. Aristarchus – who on an earlier journey had suffered at the hands of the mob at Ephesus (19:29), was also there, and shared Paul's imprisonment (Colossians 4:10).

And we must not forget the Roman centurian, Julius. He treated Paul well and trusted him when they landed at Sidon. Later on he saved Paul's life (27:43). Without Julius, Paul would not have survived. Paul would never have arrived in Rome, and some letters, Philippians, Colossians, Ephesians – perhaps also the pastoral letters to Timothy and Titus – would not have been written. Julius was Paul's warder, his prison guard, but also the means of Paul's freedom. Because of him, Paul had freedom to write and preach.

How often the least likely of our acquaintances turn out to be our truest friends! When everything seems to conspire against us we find out who our true friends are. Let us, then, value and thank God for friendship.

MAJORITY OPINION

ACTS 27:9–13 – 'Since the harbour was unsuitable to winter in, the majority decided that we should sail on . . . When a gentle south wind began to blow they thought they had obtained what they wanted' (vv. 12a,13a, NIV).

Julius was a good friend to Paul, but this did not mean that he always took notice of what Paul said. In matters of seamanship it seemed natural to take the advice of the master and crew of the vessel. When the captain advised going on from the little harbour called Fair Havens, Julius accepted this as a sensible course of action. How could he have known otherwise?

Look closely, to see a little warning sign that should have alerted him. Fair Havens was a small place, but it had been good enough to provide a decent shelter from the storm. Why, then, would it be unsuitable to winter in?

There were two hundred and seventy-six people on board the ship, most of them sailors. They didn't want to spend the winter in a little place with no night life or any of the amenities they would enjoy in a larger port like Phoenix. At Phoenix they would find the bars and the market places, the theatres and gambling dens they loved to frequent. Lulled into a false sense of security by fair weather they set out, less concerned for their safety than for the creature comforts they would miss by staying in Fair Havens. The majority are by no means always right. How often majority opinion is a mass expression of selfishness.

Paul did not need any special prophetic gift to warn them the voyage would be a disaster. An experienced traveller, more familiar with those seas than even some of the younger, inexperienced mariners, he knew what was necessary: a safe harbour rather than a pleasurable one. Question: Do we ever sacrifice long-term safety and joy in the Lord for short-term pleasure and gain?

DIVINE PROVIDENCE

ACTS 27:13–26 – ' "So keep up your courage; I trust in God that it will turn out as I have been told" ' (v. 25, NEB).

This description of the storm and shipwreck is one of the most exciting passages in the Bible and among the best written stories in all literature. Nevertheless, Luke had more than a literary purpose in mind when he wrote it. He wished to underline the way God had guided Paul, and brought him through many dangers to his destination. It confirms a truth we encounter again and again in Scripture: the 'slings and arrows of outrageous fortune' do not have the power to bring those out of God's care who keep themselves in God's will. As we may see from the life of Paul, being in God's will does not ensure immunity from danger and grief, but it does guarantee the believer's ultimate triumph.

It might surprise us that Paul's knowledge was proved to be superior to that of the ship's captain even on matters affecting the voyage. We should expect the experienced sailor to know more about seamanship than Paul did. Christians cannot expect to be regarded as experts on everything. (This is one reason why the Church should be ready to accept 'outside' advice on certain issues – about money and property, for example.)

But to those who live close to Christ there sometimes comes guidance which runs counter to the expected and which at times transcends reason (though it never does violence to it). Christians may not always understand the way God leads them, but of this they may be sure: his directions are always consistent with his love and his interest in his children's well-being.

THE BALANCED CHRISTIAN LIFE

ACTS 27:27–44 – 'Shortly before daybreak, Paul urged them all to take some food' (v. 33, NEB).

In his life of William Booth, Harold Begbie observes that the Founder of The Salvation Army has no place either among the intellectuals or the mystics. He was a practical man, he says, who was very suspicious of Christians obsessed with introspective religion. William Booth had one test, an infallible and scriptural test, for all talkers, writes Begbie. It was: 'What do you *do*?'

Nevertheless, this writer does acknowledge that there were moments in William Booth's life when he 'looked away from the mechanism of evangelisation and desired acquaintance with the large serenities of mysticism'. We might say, then, that he was a practical man who recognised the value and even the necessity of the mystic moment of prayer.

So far as Paul is concerned, we might want to put it the other way round. Mystic and thinker though he undoubtedly was, he was not, as some people are judged to be, so heavenly minded as to be of no earthly use! The apostle was also a practical man, this side of his nature being seen as he advised the hungry people on the ship to 'have something to eat'.

Our own Christianity should combine devotion and service, so that they are a balanced, unified whole. We direct our devotion to heaven, but our prayers must also embrace the needs of earth; indeed, those Christians who are most in touch with God are those who are closest to people. Jesus himself taught that as we minister to the needs of others we minister to him. To live in Christ's Spirit means to have a devoted heart and also a ready hand.

THE TRIUMPH OF THE GOSPEL

ACTS 28:16–31 – 'He stayed there two full years ... proclaiming the Kingdom of God and teaching the facts about the Lord Jesus Christ quite openly and without hindrance' (vv. 30,31, NEB).

The story Luke tells is that of a great accomplishment. The gospel had been brought from Galilee to Jerusalem (as he describes in his Gospel), and from Jerusalem to Rome (as he tells in Acts). And having given an account of Paul's arrival in the Imperial city he then concludes his record. What subsequently happened to Paul we do not certainly know, for Luke does not say, but he was surely right to end where he did – on a note of triumph, with Paul preaching the message in the most important city in the world – 'without hindrance'.

We have seen, however, that the triumph Luke describes was not achieved easily. There were setbacks, frustrations and dangers; at times it must have appeared to some Christians that the movement had little chance of success. But it *did* succeed, and in that we may all take heart, for as nothing could stop the gospel then, nothing can stop it *now*. Its triumph is assured because it is of God who is great and good.

We should note also, as we come to the end of Luke's story, that the victory of the gospel did not, and does not, rest on the success or failure of any one man, even such a man as Paul. The work of God proceeded, however, and still proceeds.

We each have our part to play in the onward march of God's truth, but the truth itself is bigger than any of us. This is Jesus himself. Paul would be the first to direct our admiration away from himself towards Christ, for it is Christ who has brought us, and indeed *is*, the gospel, and it is Christ we love and serve.

Part 7

SONGS OF ISRAEL

The Book of Psalms was compiled as a hymn book for use in the Second Temple, built after the return of the Israelites from the Babylonian captivity, around 520 BC. Like our own modern hymn books the Psalter (as this book is sometimes called) contains material written at different times, over many years, and with a variety of themes. These include trust in God; prayers to God expressing deep and urgent needs; and especially we find expressions of exultant praise. Sometimes complaints and doubts are found, and even vindictive thoughts against enemies – but always there is an upward look to God.

There is honesty here, vivid outpourings of the whole range of human emotions. And so much of what is said is still relevant. But that is not surprising. The religion of the psalms is sound – making allowances, as we must, for the times in which they were written. And the psychology is sound also, though the psalmists didn't use that word, of course. They knew a great deal about God, however, and about human nature, and neither of these changes as the years and centuries go by.

We need to remember that we can do with the psalms something the Israelites couldn't: see and use them through our Christian eyes. So, for example, when we use the greatly loved Psalm 23, 'The Lord is my shepherd', for us the Lord is Jesus, the good shepherd. When the psalmists sing about God being a Father, we remember that Jesus spoke a great deal about the Fatherhood of God, and that the word Father was often on his lips when he prayed – and he taught his followers to use the word. He took an ancient concept and gave it new and deeper meaning.

If the psalms were precious to those who first used them, as they undoubtedly were, how much more precious they may be to us who live this side of Bethlehem!

Only a short selection can be given here – and some readers' favourites may not be included – but the various commentators focus on the chosen psalms' abiding value and show what marvellous things are here for us – to hearten, challenge and express, no doubt, some of our own hopes, needs and praise better than we ever could.

Someone has said that the psalms are 'manna for the soul'. May this be true for all who read these comments!

ROSES ALL THE WAY?

PSALM 1 – 'In all that he does, he prospers' (v. 3, RSV).

What an appealing picture the psalmist gives of the results of righteous living! The good man, delighting in God's will, prospers in all he does! But we all know that life is not like that! Even for the servants of God it is not roses all the way. Elsewhere in the psalms – the 73rd provides an example – there are bitter complaints at the prosperity of the wicked in contrast to the sorrows and misfortunes of the righteous. The prophet Malachi laments that 'evildoers not only prosper, but when they put God to the test, they escape' (3:15).

Good men and women have never found that serving God faithfully brings immunity from suffering. The young bride of missionary John Paton died in childbirth, and the baby a few days later. Far from friends, the broken-hearted servant of God dug a grave and lovingly buried his dead with his own hands. But the assurance of God's presence never left him, and despite his broken heart he could say, 'I was not altogether forsaken. The ever-merciful Lord sustained me.'

When we read this psalm through in the light of the revelation of God's love that Christ brought – and we should read the Old Testament in no other way – we are assured that the psalmist is right. Whatever comes the way of the good man and woman, there is sure and lasting fellowship with the God of love and mercy. It is in the way of unrighteousness that the seeds of sorrow and death are found – as the psalmist knew (vv. 4–6).

WHEN GOD SEEMS ABSENT

PSALM 6 – 'How long, O Lord, how long? Turn, O Lord, and deliver me; save me because of your unfailing love' (vv. 3,4, NIV).

'The author of the universe is hard to find,' said Plato. 'In finding God you must have as much patience as a man who sits by the seaside and undertakes to empty the ocean, lifting one drop of water with a straw,' said Mahatma Gandhi. The psalmist was certainly not as pessimistic about the religious search as these men. Yet he was perplexed by God's apparent slowness in coming to his aid. His cry, 'How long, O Lord?' highlights a painful experience which comes to most believers at some time.

When God seems absent we should ponder every past experience of his presence. It has been well said that 'he who has heard God's voice can bear God's silence'. When Pascal died they found sewn into his jacket a scrap of parchment recording one supreme hour of communion. A few broken phrases told of the peace and certitude of that experience – 'joy, joy, joy, floods of joy'. Probably there was no second experience like that for Pascal but he lived the rest of his life by the certainty which that hour gave him.

When God seems absent we should look for the cause in ourselves rather than in God. Most likely our own variable emotions, or even our physical condition, have dimmed our spiritual awareness. Perhaps we need to repent of some disobedience or failure. Whatever the cause, we should reassure ourselves that God's love for us is constant and, even when we cannot feel his presence, he is with us just the same.

WE COUNT WITH GOD

PSALM 8 – 'When I consider your heavens, the work of your fingers, the moon and the stars, which you have set in place, what is man that you are mindful of him?' (vv. 3,4, NIV).

Albert Einstein once wrote of his 'humble admiration of the illimitably superior spirit who reveals himself in the silent details we are able to perceive with our frail and feeble minds', a modern expression of the psalmist's conviction that the creation is a declaration of God's glory. But what amazed the psalmist most of all was man's position in creation – a 'little less than God' (v. 5).

We might well share the psalmist's amazement as we consider the vastness of creation, of which we have greater knowledge than he could ever have had. He did not know that the earth is millions of years old; modern science tells us it is. He did not know, as we do, that our sun is only one among millions of stars in our galaxy and that there are millions of galaxies spread out in inconceivable distances.

Can we really have significance? The psalmist saw that God's relationship to man is of a higher order than his relationship to the stars. That the world is a speck in the universe and man a speck among the mountains, forest and plains of the earth is irrelevant. Size is no guarantee of importance. The mountaineer's small son is of more value than the towering mountain he finds pleasure in scaling.

The message of the psalmist is: We are made in God's image; the life of God is within us; in a special way we count. Christians know this, for in Christ the divine concern has been demonstrated unmistakably.

ATHEISM – ANCIENT AND MODERN

PSALM 14 – 'The fool says in his heart, "There is no God"'
(v. 1, RSV).

Atheism, as an intellectual denial of God's existence, was unknown to
the psalmist. Practical godlessness, showing itself in utter disregard
of the rights of others, is what he describes. The word translated
'fool' denotes moral perversity, not mere ignorance or weakness of
reason.

The cause of much intellectual atheism is a distorted picture of
God. A schoolgirl was shocked when a classmate said her mother
did not believe in God. Her wise teacher said, 'We don't tell other
people what they ought to believe, Helen . . . It's not our business.
Besides, we don't know *which* God Cicely's mother doesn't believe
in. Perhaps I don't believe in him, either. It isn't the word "God"
that matters, but what you mean when you use it.'

Describing his early loss of faith, Jean-Paul Sartre records some
youthful mischief. 'I was busy covering up my crime,' he wrote, 'when
God saw me. I felt his gaze inside my head and on my hands; I turned
round and round in the bathroom, horribly visible, a living target.'
His indignation at this prying, accusing 'God' caused him finally to
reject religion. He later said of God, as an elderly person might say
of an 'old flame', 'Fifty years ago, without that misunderstanding,
without that mistake, without the accident which separated us, there
might have been something between us.'

Atheists are often people who have rightly dismissed an infantile
picture of God, but have never taken the trouble to examine the
mature claims of faith. A prayer: God of love, may my life so reflect
your goodness that others will find it easier to believe in you.

HOW GOD WORKS

PSALM 17 – 'You know my heart. You have come to me at night; you have examined me completely and found no evil desire in me' (v. 3, GNB).

The writer of this psalm was a man in whom nobility of soul and pettiness of mind seemed strangely mingled. Pleading for divine help, he accepted that God was the best judge of his conduct and character, yet was at pains to impress him with how good he was. He claimed that 'I speak no evil as others do' (v. 4), but proceeded to ask for severe punishment for his enemies. Though obviously a sincere seeker, he is in this psalm revealed in a poor light.

Two main points emerge for our consideration. Our expectation of God's help in this situation or that must be based on his love for us and not on any merit we think we may possess. The truth is that we have nothing save our love to offer him. Again, it is always a mistake, though a common one, to assume that our trust in God merits his special consideration. We cannot demand that God intervene in our circumstances and at the same time expect to live in a world of dependable natural laws. This is not to say miracles cannot happen, only that we cannot claim them as a right.

But, while we may not demand exemption *from* life's pains, we may expect protection *in* them. And we should remember that if the common experiences of life, including its suffering, heighten our spiritual perception, good will have come out of them.

Wrote Evelyn Underhill: 'It is in the ordinary pain and joy, tension and self-oblivion, sin and heroism of normal experience that his moulding and transforming work is known.'

WE SEE THE LORD

PSALM 19 – 'Nothing can hide from its heat' (v. 6, GNB).

When C.S. Lewis describes Psalm 19 as 'the greatest poem in the Psalter and one of the greatest lyrics in the world,' we are encouraged to look at these fourteen verses particularly closely.

The psalm tells of two places where its author found God. The glories of the heavens testified to the handiwork of their Creator. Across the barriers of continent and language sounded the harmony of the heavens – in Joseph Addison's words:

> *For ever singing, as they shine,*
> *'The hand that made us is divine.'*

The psalmist also saw that God revealed himself in Scripture. Even more wonderful than the revelation of God's glory in the heavens was the revelation of his will in his word. Burning and penetrating it might be, like the sun, but with a heat that quickened and educated the heart.

This was proved by Anthony Bloom. As a sceptical youth, antagonistic to Christianity, he once turned to Mark's Gospel to see if it sustained what a priest had been saying. 'Before I reached the third chapter,' he wrote, 'I became aware of a presence. I saw nothing. I heard nothing . . . It was a simple certainty that I was in the presence of him whose life I had begun to read with such revulsion.'

Those today who would see the Lord will find he is not left without witnesses. May the Spirit touch our eyes and make us to see!

UNFAILING CARE

PSALM 23 – 'The Lord is my shepherd, I shall lack nothing' (v. 1, NIV).

This must be the best known psalm in the Psalter. Because of that, there must be also a great danger of allowing its words to pass through the mind without finding any lodging place in thought.

Although it is frequently referred to as the 'Shepherd psalm', it will be noticed that only verses 1 to 4 are concerned with that theme. Verse 5 describes what a generous host prepares for a guest, and the last verse sums up the psalmist's confidence in God. The whole psalm speaks of God's care and protection, and it is that aspect which has endeared it to readers through the ages.

Alexander MacLaren, the great Scottish preacher, said, 'The world could spare many a large book better than this sunny little psalm. It has dried many tears and supplied the mould into which many hearts have poured their peaceful faith.'

The psalmist is not chiefly concerned with his troubles and afflictions, but they do become part of the poem that he writes. That is important, for it stresses the fact that God's presence provides succour in suffering and not immunity from it. To help us reflect upon this divine care it might be helpful to consider some aspects of a shepherd's work as described in Isaiah 40:11: 'He gathers the lambs in his arms and carries them close to his heart; he leads those that have young.'

The ultimate in divine protection is seen in Jesus who said, 'I am the good shepherd. The good shepherd lays down his life for the sheep' (John 10:11). To such care we can confidently commit ourselves.

WHERE GOD LIVES

PSALM 26 – 'I love the house where you live, O Lord, the place where your glory dwells' (v. 8, NIV).

In this psalm we find protestations of personal goodness which seem to border on self-righteousness. This and passages of a similar kind in other psalms result from the psalmists' contrasting their own sincerity and innocence with the hypocrisy and wickedness of those who opposed them. When they measured their own defects by the standards of God's holiness the result was very different. The latter course is always spiritually safer.

The psalmist's love of God's house was in reality a love of God's presence, for the idea that God was specially present in the temple persisted throughout Old Testament times. It is worth noting, however, that from the earliest times the Jews thought their God less localised than the gods of surrounding nations. Unlike the Baal shrines, the Ark of the Covenant could be carried from place to place. This was but the beginning of a long process in which the idea of God's presence was gradually freed from all restrictions to a particular place.

There is no place where God is not. To experience his presence we need not retreat into a particular place but must rather perceive the religious dimension in every part of our lives. When writing in his journal John Wesley records, 'God was before me all the day long. I sought and found him in every place; and could truly say, when I lay down at night, Now I have *lived* a day.'

John Robinson wrote: 'We have got to learn that the "House of God" is the world in which God lives, not the contractor's hut set up in the grounds.'

GOD-CENTRED CONFESSION

PSALM 32 – 'Blessed is he whose transgressions are forgiven, whose sins are covered' (v. 1, NIV).

The psalmist's description of the bliss of forgiveness (v. 1) is followed by the acknowledgment that this bliss can be experienced only by those in whose spirit there is no deceit (v. 2). In other words, the condition of forgiveness is absolute sincerity, which involves confession.

The psalmist illustrates this from his own experience, drawing a moving picture of his misery while he refused to admit his guilt. Notice, though, that God never left him to himself; the psalmist was always aware of the divine hand upon him (v. 4) which, commented A.F. Kirkpatrick, made itself felt, 'partly by the remorse of conscience, partly perhaps by actual sickness. He suffered and complained, but such complaint was no prayer and brought no relief while he would not confess his sin'.

Here, then, is underlined the necessity for confession, and confession requires self-examination, something in which many of us fear to engage. Plato said that 'the unexamined life is not liveable for a human being', a saying with which A.M. Ramsey says he agrees, while admitting that he feels many people may object to it. He points out, therefore, that confession does not mean being introspective, conducting a sort of spiritual flea-hunt about our character and conduct, but means 'looking towards God'. Confession, he says, 'begins in thankfulness . . . in the contemplation of God, in his greatness as our Creator, in his greatness as our Saviour'.

Now, if healthy self-examination and confession must be God-centred we must look to God continually. Like the prophet (Isaiah 6) we shall then certainly see ourselves as we really are, but having first seen him who is love we shall not be daunted, but with gratitude accept the pardon he is ready to bestow.

NO NEED TO PRETEND

PSALM 38 – 'O Lord, you know what I long for; you hear all my groans . . . Help me now, O Lord my Saviour' (vv. 9,22, GNB).

The state of the man described in verses 1–14 of this psalm is almost too much for our imagination. In addition to his extreme physical suffering he is deserted by friends, weighed down by his sin, and persecuted by his enemies.

This does not prevent him from pouring out the agony of his soul before God. Many of us who have been brought up within the traditional reserve of Western culture do not express our inner feelings very readily. It is not the done thing to show the anger and resentment we feel. With that attitude there comes the tendency to be less than frank before God. He must have special reverence and we must not complain.

We need only to stop and think for a moment to recognise just how ridiculous this attitude is. God, by his very nature, knows our deepest needs and we cannot hide our true feelings from him. The psalmist recognises this (v. 9), but he still pours out his complaints.

If God knows so much about us why do we need to be so frank with him? Because there can be deep harmful effects in locking our real feelings away. At the very least we create a barrier between ourselves and God – we shut ourselves off from his help. At worst, we could create an emotional time bomb which could explode later – with devastating results. No matter how reserved we may be, there is no point in trying to pretend when we approach God.

WHERE TRUE RICHES LIE

PSALM 39 – 'Man is a mere phantom as he goes to and fro. He bustles about only in vain; he heaps up wealth, not knowing who will get it . . . My hope is in you' (vv. 6,7, NIV).

The problem of why the wicked prosper is the background of this psalm as it is of others. But here there is a difference in attitude. The psalmist compares his lot with that of evil men but now finds relief, not in prayers for their punishment, as he sometimes does, but in his own communion with the divine.

His situation still causes him concern, but he asks that he might be helped to face the fact of his mortality and find his hope only in God. An understanding of the frailty of human life and a recognition of the folly of envying the prosperous would help him stifle selfish thoughts.

Is there not something here for us to note? If our treasure is 'in heaven', as Jesus said (Matthew 6:19,20), it must be foolish to make a fuss about earthly possessions and a contradiction of our Christian commitment to get caught up in the rush for *things* which characterises a large slice of twentieth-century life.

Notice the sadness of this psalm; the writer had no sure belief in an after-life. The best he could hope for was that he might live on in his children when he himself entered Sheol, the shadowy place of the dead, and he asks, 'Let me smile again, before I go away and cease to be' (v. 13, NEB).

It was a mark of courage and faith that without a 'sure and certain hope' he still trusted God. Our faith has a deeper base, yet do we show, by a hopeful approach to life's problems, that we have grasped the significance of the risen, loving Lord?

SPREADING THE NEWS

PSALM 45 – 'I will perpetuate your memory through all generations; therefore the nations will praise you for ever and ever' (v. 17, NIV).

This psalm was probably written to celebrate the marriage of an Israelite king, perhaps that of Solomon to the daughter of the king of Egypt (see 1 Kings 3:1). Whatever its original purpose, however, Christian tradition sees the psalm as symbolising the union of Christ with his people. On this basis let us take two ideas in the psalm and apply them to our own Christian commitment.

The first is this: our union with Christ means our obedient devotion to his will. The word addressed to the bride, 'Forget your own people and your father's house' (v. 10), recall Christ's saying, 'Anyone who wants to be my follower must love me far more than he does his own father, mother, wife, children, brothers, or sisters' (Luke 14:26, LB).

The divine demand is stern and far-reaching, but absolute devotion to Christ is the only way to the deep joy which is his will for us. Is it our reluctance to submit, born of a misunderstanding of the purpose of submission, that robs us of our Christian joy?

The second idea to note and apply is that our union with Christ involves us in a responsibility for spreading the gospel. This is suggested by verse 17, highlighted above. Here is a task to which we must positively address ourselves, banishing any ideas that confronting people with Christ might be an unwarranted intrusion into privacy. When a European once expressed the opinion that Christian missions had been a disaster for Africa, a highly educated African said to him, 'I'm surprised to hear you say that. You know, if it hadn't been for Christian missions I should probably be eating you now!'

How seriously do we take our responsibility for 'spreading the news'?

PERSONAL FELLOWSHIP WITH GOD

> PSALM 51 – 'Create a pure heart in me, O God, and give me a new and steadfast spirit' (v. 10, NEB).

In this, the profoundest of the 'penitential psalms', we see how far Hebrew thought has progressed from the old idea of spirit being 'wind' and 'breath'. The psalmist begs for a 'pure heart', which is another way of saying a 'new and right spirit' (v. 10, RSV). Here there is no possibility of mass hysteria or brain-washing; we are allowed a glimpse of a soul alone with God, and it is curious that those who seek to explain away the reality of religious faith generally ignore such prayers as these.

It is true that the author does not distinguish his own 'spirit' from the 'Spirit' of God. Hebrew script would allow no sleight of hand with capital letters! In technical language we have here no 'doctrine of the personality of the Holy Spirit' such as Christian thinkers have developed. But God is seen as acting personally, through his Spirit, upon the moral and mental life of the believer.

The traditional setting of the psalm is in the life of David after he had sinned with Bathsheba, but in truth, like all great literature, it speaks to the condition of every generation. Here the spirit is no longer an impersonal, irresistible force: no longer 'I and it', but 'I and thou'.

Thus, for any faith in God as a living personal reality, some doctrine of the Spirit is crucial. When we say that God's Spirit witnesses with our spirit, we are saying simply that God talks to us as friend to friend. Let us make the psalmist's prayer our own: 'Create a pure heart in me, O God, and give me a new and steadfast spirit. Grant the same blessing to . . .'

STUDY IN CONTRASTS

PSALM 52 – 'But like an olive green am I, living within the house of God' (v. 8, JM).

'It is rare to find a psalmist denouncing an individual,' comments Joseph Gelineau, 'and somewhat disconcerting.' The problem is lessened if the psalm is an example of the 'threatening oracles' pronounced by prophets during religious festivities. The figure here addressed would then exemplify a type, not a particular person. Two ways of life would be portrayed before the congregation to help them evaluate their own lives more truly.

Lying and mischief-making are here regarded as particularly blameworthy. We may recall the story of Aesop whose master ordered him on successive occasions to prepare the most perfect, and the most abominable, dish on earth. Each time Aesop produced a dish of tongue, saying that the first tongue speaks the most beautiful thoughts and poems and, on the second occasion, that it was the instrument of falsehood and misrepresentation. Neither the childlike quality of this fable, nor the strong language of the psalmist should lead us to forget that sins of the tongue are ones we more easily excuse, yet they are frequently the most destructive of human happiness

Two lively pictures the psalmist leaves us. The lying mischief-maker will be like a man snatched up from his tent: the man trusting in God like a well-rooted tree in the house of God. To this day olives grow in the temple precincts. Living in the spirit of praise and worship makes our speech both kind and fruitful.

SPIRITUAL PLENITUDE

PSALM 63 – 'On my bed I remember you, I think of you through the watches of the night' (v. 6, NIV).

Some commentators who set the psalms in the context of the temple liturgy suggest that this psalm, expressing the need of a Davidic king and his loyal people, may have been used as the king prepared for sleep at the sanctuary in quest of a revelation. The psalmist strikingly contrasts the wilderness experience in which God is felt to be far removed (v. 1) with the spiritual plenitude of communion with God. 'In verses 4 to 9 the images accumulate: to love God is to live fully, to feast, to rest content, to be under a protecting wing, to embrace and to be embraced.' So comments Joseph Gelineau, adding that even the mystical poet St John of the Cross could scarcely do better than this.

There is more here than poetry, however. The psalmist's claim that his thoughts turned godward 'in the night watches' (AV) or 'at dawn' (Knox), is starkly practical in this hectic age. Where do our thoughts turn when we lie sleepless upon our beds or when we first awake?

'During years of sickness when I could not sleep for pain,' wrote Nels Ferre, 'I discovered the joy and strength of praying at night. Like the monks who used to get up at various times during the night to worship God, I would lie back letting myself sink into God. Too weary to struggle, throwing my spent self on the Holy Spirit, I experienced real rest and an unmistakable inflow of power.'

NEARNESS TO GOD

PSALM 73:1–17 – 'I envied the arrogant when I saw the prosperity of the wicked' (v. 3, NIV).

Here in this psalm we meet again the problem that exercised the thinking of many in Old Testament times: Why do the wicked prosper? The psalmist says here that his faith had all but given way as he looked upon unrighteous men who appeared to enjoy immunity from trouble and pain, while he, a servant of God, did not escape them. He obviously expected that his own piety should be rewarded, and the pride and blasphemies of the wicked should be punished. In this he betrayed the shallowness of his thinking.

If a man practises religion to find prosperity and happiness, he is really trying to use God for his own selfish ends, when he should be worshipping God for no other reason than that God is love and truth. There are those today, even with the fuller revelation of God's purposes we possess in Christ, who reveal the same wrong thinking when they cry, after some disaster has overtaken them: 'Why did this happen to me? I have always tried to be good.' We may not know why it happened, and the mystery continues to perplex us after we have searched our Bible for some easy answer. What the Bible does, however, is show us a loving God who himself is not immune from suffering, and in him we are exhorted to trust.

The perplexed psalmist eventually came to the place where he found, as J.H. Eaton writes, that 'the centre of all is his nearness to God', and he revalued everything accordingly. And it is on our own 'nearness to God' that our assessment of our own painful condition depends. Then our situation becomes not merely bearable, but powerless to rob us of our peace.

THE SHAME OF SELFISH PRAYERS

PSALM 83 – 'Let them know that you, whose name is the Lord – that you alone are the Most High over all the earth' (v. 18, NIV).

The background of this psalm was obviously some troubled period of Israel's history. Perhaps an invasion by some cruel foe was expected, and the psalmist was expressing concern about the threatened danger. But his prayer that his enemies might be scattered and that they might 'ever be ashamed and dismayed' (v. 17) probably shocks us. It is certainly out of harmony with the Spirit of Jesus.

But, to be fair, we must look at such prayers against the background of the barbarous times in which they were uttered. It was then the expected thing to treat your enemies horribly. And, furthermore, it is surely hypocritical of us to profess shock at such words as these in view of some of the atrocities committed in our own day 'in the cause of freedom', and 'from military necessity'. Our own record, after twenty centuries of Christianity, should temper our expressions of surprise at the low morality of a people without our advantages.

The point to be kept in mind, however, is that the vindictive prayers were the reaction of a people whose God had been dishonoured. These were not on the whole selfish prayers; they were made in passionate defence of his name. 'Cover their faces with shame so that men will seek your name, O Lord' (v. 16), the psalmist cried.

There may be something here for us to ponder. Are our own prayers rooted in high regard for God, or do they reflect our selfishness? G. Campbell Morgan wrote: 'Selfishness sings no songs, and sees no visions. On the other hand, a passion for the glory of God is capable of great sternness, as well as of great tenderness.'

OUR TRUE SECURITY

PSALM 91 – 'Because his love is set on me, I will deliver him; I will lift him beyond danger, for he knows me by my name' (v. 14, NEB).

In face of the indisputable fact that many of God's saints have suffered cruel pain and tragic death, how are we to view this psalm? It claims that those who live under the shadow of the Almighty God shall be safe from 'raging tempests', the 'pestilence that stalks in darkness' and the 'plague raging at noonday'. It says that no disaster shall befall them nor any calamity come upon their homes.

But the truth is that these very things have happened again and again to devout and lovely people whose trust was firmly placed in God, and whose lives were totally committed to his cause.

Furthermore, when we put these verses alongside much of what Jesus said we find a marked difference in emphasis. He made it abundantly clear that adversity, tribulation and suffering would be experienced by his followers. What, then, can this psalm say to us? It seems to contradict not only our own experience but also the very words of Jesus.

We must see this psalm as beautifully portraying the *spiritual* security of those who belong to Christ. We may read it and take heart from it, not because it assures us of material prosperity and immunity from suffering, but because it expresses the truth so plainly underlined in the New Testament – that the *ultimate* safety of those who serve God *is* assured.

To expect God to rescue us from every physical danger is to have an immature faith. Our protection operates in the secret places of the soul and, because we are spiritual beings, that is where it really counts.

THE FOLLY OF THE HARDENED HEART

PSALM 95 – 'O that today you would harken to his voice! Harden not your hearts' (vv. 7,8, RSV).

What a contrast there is between the first and last verses of this psalm! It starts in joyful praise, and ends in anger. The two sections seem to sit awkwardly together. The key to the change in tone is found in the verse highlighted above.

It is easy to exaggerate, but isn't it true that nothing receives greater condemnation in Scripture than 'hardening the heart'? What begins as an exciting adventure, full of hope and expectation becomes soured and dull when this hardening occurs. The Israelites, with hearts hardened against Moses, were condemned to wander for a whole generation, as verse 11 points out.

This attitude of apathy, or more active stubbornness, is often understandable. A teenager may make scores of job applications, all without success. What is more natural than for that young person's heart to be hardened against society? A homeless family may find that the only way to get a roof over their heads is to part, to split up. Is it not understandable for them to become hard? But such hardness is counter-productive. It makes it even more difficult to get out of a hopeless situation. In the end they seem to be being punished for their very attitude.

Words of comfort alone cannot break through the hardening. Action is needed: costly action like that of Moses who risked everything for his stubborn people; action like that of Jesus who gave everything for those who rejected him. Unless Christians follow their Master's example a hardhearted generation who have every reason to be such, will be destroyed, wandering in a wilderness of joblessness, homelessness and – tragically – hopelessness.

REJOICING IN JUDGMENT

PSALM 96 – 'He will judge the world in righteousness and the peoples in his truth' (v. 13, NIV).

In his book, *Reflections on the Psalms*, C.S. Lewis remarks on the surprise he had when he first noticed how the psalmists talk about the judgment of God: they find judgment an occasion for *rejoicing*. He gives instances of this, one of which is found in this psalm. 'Let the heavens rejoice . . . when he comes to judge'.

C.S. Lewis says that the ancient Jew regarded the prospect of judgment as good news because it was for him as a plaintiff a privilege *to get a hearing*. It was not always easy for a man to go to court to plead for justice in some civil cases if he did not have money or influence. So, while 'Christians cry to God for mercy instead of justice [the psalmists] cried to God for justice instead of injustice'.

The Christian's view of God's judgment is profound, and C.S. Lewis thinks 'safer for our souls than the Jewish', but there is much in the Jewish conception. It brings before us a picture of a God who as a Judge will listen to men and who will be just. We should never lose sight of the consequences of sin (which is why Lewis thinks the Christian picture is 'safer') but nor must we forget the character of the Judge, and his desire for our highest well-being.

We may not be able to share the psalmist's exultation even when we understand his Jewish outlook, but it would be wrong for us to fear the divine judgment. We may rest on the truth that God loves us, a truth Jesus made unmistakably clear.

FORGIVENESS AND LOVE

PSALM 103:1–12 – 'Bless the Lord, my soul, and forget none of his benefits. He pardons all my guilt and heals all my suffering' (vv. 2,3, NEB).

The psalmist makes a list of the benefits bestowed upon him by a gracious God, and right at the top he places the blessing of forgiveness. 'He pardons all my guilt', he says as he rejoices.

The Bible makes it abundantly clear that forgiveness is man's basic need, but this fact will come home only as men realise the enormity of sin, a truth that is not easily or sufficiently appreciated. Martin Luther said that 'the recognition of sin is the beginning of salvation', sin, that is, not simply as something we *do* or *fail to do*, but as what we *are*.

It is a condition, it becomes part of our nature and its effects are irreversible save in the pity and mercy of God. He forgives those who truly want his forgiveness, and forgiveness is the only answer to human sin. We cannot expiate it; we cannot earn the remission of its penalty; we can only *accept* divine forgiveness.

Small wonder, then, that the psalmist should place the pardoning of sin at the head of all the benefits for which he wishes to thank God. And, similarly, the knowledge that our sins are forgiven and the deepest need of our heart is met, should create in us a true gratitude and move us toward God in love. We should remember, as someone has said, that we are not forgiven because we love; we love because we are forgiven.

UTILITY RELIGION

PSALM 121 – 'I lift up my eyes to the hills – where does my help come from? My help comes from the Lord, the Maker of heaven and earth' (vv. 1,2, NIV).

The Authorised Version translation, in which our help seems to come from the hills (v. 1), is wrong. That could have signified devotion to the baals of the Canaanite high places (as in 'Shall I look to the mountain gods for help?' – LB). It might have meant the worship of nature itself; but the psalmist immediately shows nature to be only the creation of 'the Lord' (v. 2).

'Lifting my eyes to the hills' could indicate a looking up to the temple and the Holy City with a reliance on ritual, but the rest of the psalm expresses a warm personal awareness in the pilgrim of a caring, immediate God. Or we might picture *ourselves* in a valley of danger or depression, and make this a yearning cry for deliverance from our circumstances. But the hills are incidental; just a focus and perspective for the pilgrim's desire. He is, in fact, admitting his heavy dependence on God.

Do *we* not need to abandon our attempts at self-sufficiency and confess loud and often, 'My help comes from the Lord'? J.S. MacArthur writes, 'Prayer means to many a sort of insurance policy . . . an *occasional* appeal to God . . . when things get really bad.' He calls this 'utility religion'. 'When we buy . . . a vacuum cleaner . . . a TV set, we are given a guarantee . . . which enables us to call upon the makers . . . if anything goes wrong . . . We are too apt to think of God like that, as someone to put things right when they go wrong, but whom we may forget so long as things are not going wrong.' The psalmist is confessing his *constant* need of God.

'O JERUSALEM!'

PSALM 122 – 'I rejoiced with those who said to me, "Let us go to the house of the Lord." Our feet are standing in your gates, O Jerusalem . . . built like a city that is closely compacted together' (vv. 1–3, NIV).

The pilgrim, on his way to Jerusalem, at last reaches the top of the hill. He remembers his gladness when the trip was arranged. It's been hard going but (O Jerusalem!) it's all been worth it! J.S. Stewart says that Jerusalem meant three things to the pilgrim making his journey there: (a) History – 'David the shepherd-king . . . Solomon in all his glory . . . Hezekiah who had seen Sennacherib's invasion roll thunderously up to the very walls only to be halted there . . . the years of foreign domination . . . the thrilling hour of national resurrection.' (b) Religion – 'Jerusalem meant the temple and the temple meant God.' (c) Home – 'If I forget thee, O Jerusalem, let my right hand forget her cunning.'

For the Christian, too, 'the house of the Lord' is precious. It is his link with Christian, even national, history; the focus of his communal religious observance; a centre of social intercourse. But even given these three, it may still only evoke nostalgia and sentiment. We may go there often and not meet with God.

Christian pilgrims must go further and find the presence of the living God, whether there or elsewhere. 'O Jerusalem!' must become 'O God!' Even Solomon admitted: 'The highest heaven cannot contain thee; how much less this house that I have built!' (1 Kings 8:27).

God can be found in the individual consciousness, in the company of good people, in the world of nature, in the universe of the spirit. However valuable God's house and what takes place there, that must not be our only place of meeting with him.

PEACEFUL AS A BABY

PSALM 131 – 'I am content and at peace. As a child lies quietly in its mother's arms, so my heart is quiet within me' (v. 2, GNB).

How strange that the child in its mother's arms should be the picture of contentment, seeing that it has not the strength to stand, cannot find its own food, and has no defence against attack. Its contentment springs entirely from its mother's care and from not being too aware of life's dangers. Contentment and calm spring from trust.

There is an old story of a Christian military officer and his wife caught in a storm at sea. She was very alarmed and said, 'How can you keep so calm?' He pointed his sword at her throat and asked, 'Why are you not afraid?' 'Because I know you love me too well to hurt me,' she said. 'Well, I know that God loves us too much to allow any *final* harm to come to us.' Someone has said that it is all right in a calm to be a strong man in a weak boat, but in a storm it is better to be a weak man in a strong boat!

'Pride' and 'arrogance' (v. 1) destroy contentment. An *over*-concentration on the dangers of life, or a flippant arrogance about our own ability to cope with them, robs us of peace. John Hutton has written, 'It is . . . when we keep our eyes upon the bare facts of life without the light and reinforcement of faith . . . when we turn our eyes away from the sky, when we suspect the song and the dream (instead of trusting them), that the circumstances of the human lot seem harsh and dreary and desperate.'

GOD, MIGHTY AND HOLY

PSALM 150 – 'Praise God in his sanctuary . . . for his acts of power; praise him for his surpassing greatness' (vv. 1,2, NIV).

To be able to speak of holiness and power in the same breath is by no means common. Thomas Aldrich wrote: 'The possession of unlimited power will make a despot of almost any man. There is a possible Nero in the gentlest human creature.'

In ancient tales about so-called *gods* there is little suggestion that they were holy, or even moral. And today we are sometimes surprised when we hear of someone who has power to feather his own nest and does not do so. There is not necessarily any goodness, on the other hand, in the man who is good only because he does not have the opportunity to be anything else.

A.C. Dixon makes a helpful distinction between influence and power: 'Moody . . . began without influence, he became influential through power . . . and the power of Moody's life was *God himself* at work. Jesus was not a man of influence (he made himself of no reputation) but of power. Paul and Silas did not have influence enough to keep out of gaol; but they had power enough to shake the doors open and walk out.'

Perhaps it is only when we are released from the power of influence for our own sake that we can be filled with true spiritual power; and holiness into the bargain!

Holy, holy, holy, Lord God Almighty!
All thy works shall praise thy name in earth and sky and sea;
Holy, holy, holy, merciful and mighty,
God in three Persons, blessed Trinity!

Hallelujah! Praise the God of power *and* holiness!

Part 8

THE TEACHING
OF THE EARLY CHURCH

The New Testament consists of (a) five pieces of narrative – the four Gospels and the Acts of the Apostles; (b) one mysterious and highly symbolic work – the Revelation of John (part of which we are to look at in the final section of this book); and (c) twenty-one letters, some addressed to churches, others to individuals. Thirteen of these letters are by the apostle Paul (though there are scholars who question the Pauline authorship of some of these), and the other eight are by various writers: James (one letter), Peter (two), John (three), Jude (one) and someone unknown (one, the letter to the Hebrews). In this section we are going to look at some of these letters and their teaching and consider what they have to say to us today.

Many of them were written before the first of the Gospels, Mark, though the faith was being preached before anyone put pen to paper to make a record. The letters were written to address immediate, local situations: to deal with problems that had arisen about matters of belief and conduct; to answer questions being put to the leadership by puzzled believers; sometimes to issue rebuke for wrong behaviour. The letter to the Romans appears to be the only one that presents Paul's thought in a systematic way.

The letters are invaluable as a guide to how the early leaders were thinking about and interpreting the faith. Such high value was placed on them that they were kept and no doubt referred to again and again as the Christians came together for prayer and worship. Many years later they were incorporated into the Christian Scriptures when the contents of these were being decided upon. Paul and the others would possibly have been surprised at this: they had not been writing *Scripture*, but simply giving counsel, addressing specific, local issues.

We now have these letters as part of our Bible, and what Paul said to Timothy about the only Scriptures the Christians then had – the Old Testament – can be applied to our enlarged Bible. He wrote: 'All Scripture is God-breathed and is useful for teaching, rebuking, correcting and training in righteousness, so that the man of God may be thoroughly equipped for every good work' (2 Timothy 3:16,17, NIV).

The letters are not arranged chronologically in the New Testament but, while the timing is much debated, those on which comments are made here are given in the *possible* order of their appearance.

GREAT CHRISTIAN CONCEPTS

1 THESSALONIANS 1:1–5 – 'We always thank God for all of you, mentioning you in our prayers' (v. 2, NIV).

From the opening salutation, written in the common form of that day, the apostle immediately goes on to express gratitude to God for the quality of the Thessalonians' faith. Despite the difficulties of their situation they were standing fast. How that cheered him! His knowledge of their Christian witness, no doubt reported to him by Timothy who had recently returned from a visit to Thessalonica, is of particular interest. Three great Christian virtues were being demonstrated in their lives. 'Your *faith* has shown itself in action, your *love* in labour and your *hope* of our Lord Jesus Christ in fortitude' (NEB), he wrote.

Faith in action. Christian faith is not just an attitude of the mind; there is an active quality about it which issues in loving deeds. *Love in labour.* False ideas about the meaning of love constitute one of the sadder features of contemporary life. If, William Neil points out, the fault of nineteenth-century Christianity lay in a confusion of Christian charity with almsgiving, the fault of the twentieth is that the whole concept of love is being debased.

This writer affirms that 'Christian love is briefly the reproduction in our everyday affairs of Jesus's attitude to the men and women of his time.' *Hope in fortitude* denotes, not a passive patience, but that which goes on when the situation seems hopeless, not resignedly but radiantly, because it is rooted in the glorious fact of Christ. How helpful and challenging it would be to ponder these three great Christian concepts and apply them to our own lives!

THE TEACHING OF THE EARLY CHURCH

LIVING THE GOSPEL

1 THESSALONIANS 1:6–10 – 'You became imitators of us and of the Lord . . . And so you became a model to all the believers in Macedonia and Achaia' (vv. 6,7, NIV).

This passage bears striking witness to the way Christianity spreads. Paul said that he and his companions went to Thessalonica as followers of Christ; the Thessalonians themselves copied their example and other people in other places followed theirs. And so the gospel was passed from heart to heart. How effective for the kingdom of God is that Christian who really lives out his faith in everyday life!

In *Miracle on the River Kwai* Ernest Gordon tells how he entered a Japanese prisoner-of-war camp in the Second World War an unbeliever and emerged after three-and-a-half terror-filled years a convinced Christian. He began to be aware of the reality of God by observing two fellow-prisoners who were Christians – Dusty, a Methodist, and Dinty, a Roman Catholic. 'In each of them it was his faith that lent a special grace to his personality; through them both faith expressed a power, a presence, greater than themselves,' he wrote. 'I was beginning to see that life was infinitely more complex, and at the same time more wonderful, than I had ever imagined . . . God had not left us. He was with us, calling us to live in the divine fellowship. I was beginning to be aware of the miracle that God was working in the Death Camp by the River Kwai.'

Neither church services nor sermons started Ernest Gordon on the road that led to his Christian commitment – but the strong and simple faith of two men who knew and lived Christ. And only as we, by the quality of our own living bear witness to the reality and beauty of our relationship with Christ, will we be effective in encouraging others to look to him for themselves.

JUDGMENT AND PROMISE

2 THESSALONIANS 1:5–12 – 'It is surely just that God should balance the account by sending trouble to those who trouble you, and relief to you who are troubled' (v. 6, NEB).

Judgment is a constantly recurring theme of the Bible. The prophets of the Old Testament spoke about it; and so did Jesus in the New. We meet it again in this reading where Paul speaks of the justice of God's judgment and points out that 'those who will not obey the gospel . . . will suffer the punishment of eternal ruin' (vv. 8,9). He uses the language of the Old Testament, but the truth he emphasises is eternal.

Yet we must not fail to notice the mingling here of promise with judgment, for they always go together in God's dealings with us. Hope is promised to those who believe, but inevitable loss comes to those who wilfully disobey.

In one of his sermons Dr Colin Morris points out that they are false prophets who speak a simple word of Promise *or* Judgment. True prophets speak a paradoxical word of Promise *and* Judgment. 'So the truly prophetic word has moral depth. It is never flippant or casually simple because it is addressed to Man, who oscillates between extremes of pride and humility, misery and grandeur. And this word speaks Promise *and* Judgment because Man needs both to be jolted into a sense of dignity when he is grovelling in the dust, and knocked off his perch when he gets cocky and forgets he is human.'

Dr Morris points out that all Jesus's promises embodied judgment, and yet his harshest judgments offered promise. This, he says, 'is the essence of true prophecy – a word of judgment which leads men to repentance and yet embodies promise, the assurance that forgiveness is possible'. This is both challenge and comfort – as it is meant to be.

FRUIT OF THE SPIRIT

GALATIANS 5:22–26 – 'Since we live by the Spirit, let us keep in step with the Spirit' (v. 25, NIV).

The outward expression of the inner nature: this is how someone has described fruit. In the spiritual sense the definition would have much in common with the teaching of Jesus who said, 'By their fruit you will recognise them. Do people pick grapes of thornbushes, or figs from thistles?' (Matthew 7:16).

This reminds us that in verses 22 and 23 Paul is not describing a humanist charter. Any suggestion that the fruit he describes can be produced by our own efforts is a contradiction of all that the apostle has sought to express in this letter to the Galatians. To consider these verses apart from the saving work of Christ (v. 1) and the consequent gift of the Holy Spirit, is as artificial as tying fruit to a Christmas tree.

The fruit of the Holy Spirit is the expression of a living union with God. There is a strengthening of that bond in *love* and *joy*; there is a Christlike attitude to life's challenges in *peace* and *patience*; there is the fruit of true Christian fellowship in *kindness* and *goodness* and the essence of discipleship is seen in *faithfulness*, *gentleness* and *self-control* which, in this context, is Christ-control.

Such fruitfulness is possible only because Christ has enabled us to 'crucify the sinful nature' and to 'walk in the Spirit'. Paul's exhortation, 'Let us keep in step with the Spirit' underlines that which is essential if we are to bear the fruit of the Spirit.

THE BEST OF WORDS OF LIFE

EACH A PART TO PLAY

1 CORINTHIANS 12:12–31 – 'Now you are the body of Christ, and each one of you is a part of it' (v. 27, NIV).

This reading makes it clear that no Christian should be over-concerned about what he might consider the smallness of the contribution he can make to the cause of Christ in the world. As part of the Body of Christ each believer has an important part to play, and the successful functioning of the whole – the Church – depends on the faithfulness of each individual member.

There is no reason for any of us to make unhelpful comparisons with our more talented fellow-Christians; this may so easily lead to resentment and discouragement. However small our gift, however restricted (humanly speaking) our sphere of influence, our own distinctive contribution counts. A commonplace truth? It is one of which we need often to be reminded. It is required of us that first of all we develop our full potential and then apply it to the full.

George Seaver wrote of Edward Wilson of the Antarctic that he held 'with an unalterable conviction . . . that the worth of life is not to be measured by its results in achievement or success, but solely by the motive of heart and effort of the will', which is another way of saying that it is faithfulness with what we have been entrusted that really matters.

George Eliot wrote – and it is something to ponder – 'The growing good of the world is partly dependent on unhistoric acts; and that things are not so ill with you and me as they might have been, is half-owing to the number who lived faithfully a hidden life, and rest in unvisited tombs.'

LOVE INCARNATE

1 CORINTHIANS 13:1–13 – 'And now I will show you the best way of all' (12:31, NEB).

It is thought-provoking that this superb lyrical poem on love, so full of deep insight and ageless wisdom, drew its inspiration from *life*. The quality of love portrayed here by Paul, was, of course, supremely incarnated in the life of Jesus, but in a fragmentary way it must have been revealed also for the apostle in the lives of those he knew who possessed the Spirit of Jesus. The best and only comment on these verses, then, must be the story of Jesus – and of his followers.

Perhaps William Sangster's 'comment' would be Kitty Wilkinson (*Westminster Sermons*). When cholera came to Merseyside in the nineteenth century and everyone who could, fled, she became foster-mother to forty-five orphaned children and earned their keep by scrubbing other people's homes. Perhaps Bernard Watson's choice (*A Hundred Years' War*) would be Dudley Gardiner, a retired military major who worked for many years in the Calcutta slums feeding the hungry, and whose commitment to love declared 'seven day a week for as long as I can do it'. Perhaps Paul Tillich would choose Elsa Brandstrom, the daughter of an ambassador who gave a lifetime of loving to German and Russian prisoners-of-war and European refugees. Of such love Tillich wrote, 'it is in the presence of God himself. For God is love. And in every moment of genuine love we are dwelling in God and God in us' (*The New Being*).

May God show us, who also have the Spirit of Jesus, this *best way of all*!

THE PAGEANT AND THE PERFUME

2 CORINTHIANS 2:12–17 – 'Thanks be to God, who always leads us in triumphal procession in Christ and through us spreads everywhere the fragrance of the knowledge of him (v. 14, NIV).

These verses refer to a common occurrence on Roman streets. A triumphant general would parade his victorious troops, and also his prisoners and spoils. The greater the status of the prisoner, the greater the glory that accrued to the general. At every corner incense was burned at the shrines of the gods and the perfume pervaded the whole atmosphere.

Paul here makes the claim that the lives of Christians are like a pageant of triumph, not to their own glory, but to the glory of their Commander Jesus Christ (v. 14). And Christians are like the incense too (vv. 15,16). For some of the prisoners of sin the influence of Christians is like a delightful perfume, for it is a foretaste of their own acceptance of Christ. But for others it is a deadly odour signifying death at the end of the road. In Sodom and Gomorrah the gospel smells of brimstone not incense, for the inhabitants refuse to bring glory to God. But whether the message is accepted or rejected the messengers are a fragrance unto God. Bunyan once said of some Christians he knew, 'They shone, they walked like a people that carried the broad seal of heaven about them.'

An old lady called the saintly Professor Drummond to the bedside of her dying husband. 'He'll no hear ye for he's deaf,' she said, 'and he'll no see ye for he's blind, but I want him to have a breath o' ye about him afore he dies.' Our fragrance depends entirely on our nearness to Jesus, its source, yet 'God uses us to make the knowledge about Christ spread everywhere like a sweet fragrance' (v. 14, GNB).

COMPLETING OUR CONSECRATION

2 CORINTHIANS 6:14–7:1 – 'Let us therefore cleanse ourselves from all that can defile flesh or spirit, and in the fear of God complete our consecration' (v. 1, NEB).

Paul was speaking in these verses about the attitude of a Christian to people and practices opposed to the Christian faith. He called for 'separation', but we must bear in mind that his primary concern was always a separation which was 'moral and spiritual, not local' (cf. 1 Corinthians 5:10). As they were the temple of God, he said, Christians had to separate themselves from all that would defile and, on the positive side, give themselves wholly to God.

Paul's words remind us that our consecration to God is not an act done once and for all. The first act of consecration initiates a life of consecration. The deed done once becomes a spirit present at all times. Those who have once turned to God live every day with their eyes in his direction. It is in this way that they 'complete their consecration'.

The same note was sounded in 1728 when William Law, summoning people to true holy living, wrote, *A Serious Call to a Devout and Holy Life*. 'If we are to be in Christ new creatures,' he wrote, 'we must show that we are so, by having new ways of living in the world . . . If our common life is not a common course of humility, self-denial, renunciation of the world, poverty of spirit, and heavenly affection, we do not live the lives of Christians.' What is necessary, in other words, is that day by day we 'complete our consecration'.

ASTONISHING VISION

ROMANS 8:18–27 – 'The created universe waits with eager expectation for God's sons to be revealed' (v. 19, NEB).

Michelangelo did four sculptures for the tomb of Pope Julius. The figures looked unfinished 'emerging from the rough stone as though they were tearing themselves out of it with tremendous effort and pain, drawing towards an assertion of triumph which yet includes within it the agony of the created process' (David Anderson).

In similar fashion Paul here portrays the whole universe travailing and agonising for a consummation which will make sense of all that has gone before. And this fulfilment is the appearance of man; not man as we know him, divided against himself and his fellows, but man as God intends him to be.

The physical universe, then, is not merely the stage setting for the drama of man's redemption, after which it will dissolve. In the biblical view the universe will share in man's redemption. Obviously, this faith can be expressed only symbolically, not descriptively. Yet 'even now man, who by selfish exploitation can turn the good earth into a dust bowl, can by responsible trusteeship make the desert blossom like the rose; what will then the effect of a completely redeemed mankind be on the creation entrusted to his care?' (F.F. Bruce).

God's purpose in creation and redemption is vast beyond our conceiving, but even a glimpse fills us with wonder and expectation.

MORE THAN 'TOGETHERNESS'

ROMANS 12:9–21 – 'Love in all sincerity, loathing evil and clinging to the good' (v. 9, NEB).

'Deprived of society,' said Lewis Mumford, 'the ego loses any confining sense of its own proper dimensions: it swings between insignificance and infinity, between self-annihilation and world conquest . . . between the desperation of suicide and the arrogance of godhead.' Relationships help to keep people in touch with reality. Yet being *in touch with* reality is not the same thing as being *rightly related to* reality. We may seek the company of our fellows in order to exploit them or merely to escape from ourselves. Only when our relationships are permeated by love can we truly find fulfilment and wholeness of personality.

The wide spectrum of life in society is reflected in these concluding chapters of Paul's letter, and what he calls for is far more than mere 'togetherness'. Nothing less than love can be the full Christian response to God's love of us. These chapters need to be placed against Paul's hymn of love in 1 Corinthians 13. The latter is far more lyrical and poetic, but here we have a prosaic, down-to-earth exposition of what this quality means in terms of everyday situations.

We need to remember that the Christian obligation to love is not primarily concerned with emotions, although life in Christ does change the way we feel about our neighbours. At any precise moment, however, we may not be able to change our feelings, yet by God's grace we can seek to act and speak with Christian concern.

LOVING ACCEPTANCE

ROMANS 15:1–7 – 'Accept one another, then, just as Christ accepted you, in order to bring praise to God' (v. 7, NIV).

Paul rounds off his examination of Christian liberty and Christian tolerance with an appeal to the example of Christ, the free man who voluntarily bound himself for others. Then he seems to summarise all he has said concerning Christian morality in one brief exhortation, calling believers to offer each other the acceptance they have found in Christ.

This is not an attitude that should be restricted to those in the Christian community. The most Christlike men and women have shown an astonishing, and sometimes shocking, acceptance of even the worst sinners. The truly holy have this ability. Only the self-righteous are censorious and condemning. Equally remarkable, the loving acceptance of the saints is never mistaken by sinners as condoning their sins. Rather it lifts them to new aspirations.

When Charles de Foucauld visited wounded legionnaires in North Africa he was warned that the visit of a priest would be nothing more than an excuse for foolish antics. When he entered the ward he was first ignored, then treated to one of the most ribald songs of the legion. 'Thank you my friends for this musical welcome,' the priest said, 'though I am afraid you must have mistaken me for your general.'

Irreverent cartoons of devils, monks and angels had been drawn on the walls. Foucauld examined each one and made a few improvements. Lastly, he went from bed to bed showing keen personal interest in each man, yet never mentioning religion. Next Sunday, every man who could be in church was there.

PARADOX OF GRACE

EPHESIANS 2:1–10 – 'It is by grace you have been saved' (v. 5, NIV).

The heart of this passage is also Paul's gospel in a nutshell – 'By grace you are saved through trusting him.' More than most, Paul was equipped to preach salvation through trust in God's love, for his efforts to obtain righteousness had been long, arduous and fruitless. What has been described as a 'hardening of the oughteries' was familiar experience to this Pharisee long before modern medicine linked mental strain and physical illness.

We are not saved by faith, as is sometimes asserted. We are saved by grace, that is, by God's unmerited love and mercy. We receive this by abandoning all trust in our own goodness, by recognising that God loves us because of who he is, not for what we are.

The paradox of Christian experience is that trust in God's grace does not lead to moral laziness and indifference. Resting in God's unqualified love we become active in genuine goodness, which is quite different from the phoney 'good works' of those striving to keep on the right side of a God they do not love. 'What a strenuous man was Paul,' wrote W.B.J. Martin. 'His writings abound in such active verbs as "strive", "run" and "do". He can even talk of "winning" Christ (Philippians 3:8). Perhaps only the man who knows that the whole of life is a gift can muster the necessary energy to go in and possess it.'

Paul Tournier wrote: 'The elite of the gospel is not made up of the "advanced", but of poor devils who accept God's grace.'

SPIRITUAL RESOURCES

EPHESIANS 6:14–17 – 'In addition to all this, take up the shield of faith, with which you can extinguish all the flaming arrows of the evil one' (v. 16, NIV).

Though the picture is of a soldier, the idea is not so much of attack as of defence. The apostle is not *in this instance* thinking of the making of assaults on the kingdom of darkness – though this is part of Christians' responsibility, and they neglect it to their own condemnation – the thought in Paul's mind at this time was the guarding of the soul. The accoutrements of the Roman soldier, to whom he was probably chained, suggested to the apostle the spiritual equipment available to the Christian in making sure of this.

From what quarters do attacks come to the modern Christian? Some are affected by the rising tide of materialism; others by the moods of despair and defeatism in a world of many problems. Yet others feel it difficult, try as they will, not to be affected by the polluted atmosphere of a society of lowered moral standards. There is real need for a reliable defence equipment.

This, as Paul sees it, consists of truth (our own integrity); righteousness (our loyalty to God's law); peace (readiness always to declare the gospel of peace – is not attack the best form of defence?); faith (a constant look upwards to God); salvation (a recognition that there is a God who can save). And, finally, a Christian's sword is the word of God. This applies not only to the Bible, but to God's total message to us, for he has many ways of speaking. These are our resources, available to us to ensure a life of spiritual victory.

HOW DO WE MEET ADVERSITY?

PHILIPPIANS 1:12–18 – 'I want you to understand that the work of the gospel has been helped on, rather than hindered, by this business of mine' (v. 12, NEB).

Had Paul been a lesser man he might easily have looked upon his imprisonment as the end of his effective service for Christ. Instead he saw it as a stepping-stone to greater service. He met the situation positively, without resentment and self-pity, and he could write joyfully about the gospel making progress in that seemingly impossible situation.

It is said that John Ruskin was once handed an expensive silk handkerchief covered with indelible, ugly stains. He took it and, working the stains into an exquisite pattern, transformed the handkerchief out of all recognition and made it a thing of beauty – to the owner's surprise and delight.

Is it possible for us to learn to face adversity and disappointment positively, turning it to spiritual advantage? We may if we remember that God shares our perplexity, frustration and tragedy with us; that even they can become part of his redemptive purpose, contributing to our knowledge and experience of God himself. 'Where life is at its blackest, injustice at its worst and physical suffering at its extreme,' wrote Joseph Stratton, 'we find, unexpectedly, our deepest certainties about the love of God instead of its denial. Here in the darkness, the light shines. This squares up with our life where what we experience in the totality of our being often evades our limping explanations.'

KEEP ON REJOICING

PHILIPPIANS 3:1–11 – 'Finally, my brethren, rejoice in the Lord. To write the same thing to you is not irksome to me, and is safe to you' (v. 1, RSV).

There has been a great deal of discussion among scholars as to what Paul meant by 'the same thing' in the above text. It may have referred to previous warnings about disunity in the church or to the exhortation 'to rejoice' in the previous sentence. The translations by Moffatt, J.B. Phillips and in the Living Bible support the latter view.

Two points emerge. The first emphasises the necessity for us to be constantly recalling those fundamentals of our Christian faith and practice that we have received. In this case it was a reminder to continue to rejoice, but it applies equally to other truths we so easily forget.

'It is not sufficiently considered', wrote the great Dr Samuel Johnson, 'that men more frequently require to be reminded than informed.' Our quest for new truth is not only valid but necessary; nothing is more tragic than a Christian with a closed mind. Nevertheless, to follow unquestioningly every fashion of thought as it appears is certainly unwise and could be destructive. Prayerful reference to God's word will help us to keep a right balance.

Second, we have a duty not only to rejoice in the Lord, but also to spread the radiance of our faith. Though not unaware of the sorrows of life – Christians themselves are not immune from them – we possess a joy in Christ that nothing can take away. Paul's repeated exhortation to rejoice should be taken to heart by all of us. Words by James Stewart give us a thought to ponder: 'The real servant of humanity today is the man whose life breathes praise.'

ABLE TO COPE

PHILIPPIANS 4:8–13 – 'He who fills me with his dynamic power has made me able to cope in any situation' (v. 13, WB).

Paul's claim to be 'able to cope in any situation' (how arresting is William Barclay's rendering here!) would be palpably absurd were it not for the acknowledgment that this was possible only *in Christ*. The difference between a humanist view of human nature and the frank recognition of the New Testament is just here. In the face of all the evidence to the contrary, humanist thinking claims that people are sufficient in themselves to achieve full development and find happiness. The Christian, on the other hand, cannot ignore the fatal flaw in human nature and people's need for 'outside' help.

This is not to say there is no good in people. An impressive record of achievement, kindness, wisdom and sacrifice shows there is. And, of course, people cannot be wholly bad when they are able to recognise and seek after goodness. There is a 'problem' of good as well as of evil. Dr John Baillie put the truth this way: 'Human nature is not a bad thing, but a good thing gone wrong.' There are tremendous and exciting potentialities in all of us when we are humble enough to acknowledge our need of God.

No man had a more purposeful, radiant life than Paul – and he lived for Christ. This is the secret of success in *being* and in *doing*. We need not plod along in the marshlands of inadequacy and defeat, but climb the mountain of victory. Let our prayer be that we might experience in increasing measure all that Christ has to give us!

CHRIST THE RECONCILER

COLOSSIANS 1:15–23 – 'For God was pleased to have all his fulness dwell in [Christ], and through him to reconcile to himself all things' (v. 20, NIV).

This remarkable passage has been the subject of a great deal of debate among Christian thinkers and Bible interpreters. Let us consider two truths it sets out.

The first concerns the *person of Christ*. The apostle claims that Christ's relationship with God is unique, without parallel in the whole of creation. He is 'the image' of God who cannot otherwise be seen. He is not simply *part of* creation, but was before all created things, and by him all creation holds together. This is a profound thought which could occupy us for a long time. The passage gives the lie to the ancient gnostic argument that Jesus was simply a man who was raised by God to special status. It also rebukes those modern teachers who relegate Jesus to the status of a great and good man.

The second truth in this passage that we must touch on concerns the *work of Christ*. Not only are we shown who Christ *is*, but also what he *does*. He reconciles all creation to God (v. 20). There is a tragic disorder in the world; it is at variance with the divine purpose. But, through Christ, everything is brought into harmony with God the Father. And because the need is an individual need, the sacrificial love which is at the heart of God's process of redemption reaches out to the lowliest person in creation.

This was a costly business for God; it involved him in a cross, but by that cross he reveals (not *creates*) God's eternal and universal love. What a thought to ponder and to prompt to wondering adoration!

GIVE HIM OUR ATTENTION

COLOSSIANS 2:1–10 – 'Just as you received Christ Jesus as Lord, continue to live in him, strengthened in the faith as you were taught' (vv. 6,7, NIV).

That the Christian lives his life *in Christ* is a theme which recurs throughout the Pauline letters. Here the apostle purposely mixes his metaphors – 'Be rooted in him; be built in him' (NEB) – in order to bring out two distinct ideas.

Rooted refers to something completed in the past, something fixed once and for all. *Built*, however, speaks of the present steady growth of Christian character. The Colossians were tempted to engage in all kinds of wild speculations, and to seek salvation by trying to come to terms with many spiritual agencies. The apostle insists that nothing more is required for Christian growth than an increasingly close union with Christ.

Dr William Sangster asked how it is possible for us to live in Christ and Christ in us. He concluded that first we must believe in its possibility, then we must want it ardently, and finally we must deliberately open our minds to Christ's incoming.

'All our school days,' he wrote, 'our teachers urged us to "give our minds" to things. There is nothing mysterious here. It is all summarised in the word "attention". We give our mind to Christ when we attend to him; think of him; talk to him; work with him; rest with him; walk with him . . . and the more we give him our minds, the more he gives us his.'

NOT LOOKING FOR PRAISE

1 TIMOTHY 5:17–25 – 'Good deeds are obvious, or even if they are not they cannot be concealed for ever' (v. 25, NEB).

Here, in this passage, Paul deals with a whole list of practical matters: Christian leaders are to be generously supported, especially those who teach and preach; accusations against them of wrongdoing should be carefully checked, but when fault is found it should be dealt with firmly. Paul also slips in here a little personal advice for Timothy who, it appears, suffered from a stomach disorder. It was a necessary warning to the delicate young man to take care of his health. He should not imagine he could serve God better with either a flabby or a wasted constitution.

In the final words of this section of his letter the apostle warns Timothy against looking for commendation and rewards for service, and also against becoming embittered when unscrupulous ones seem to succeed. It is human enough for all of us to seek recognition, and to be disappointed when it is not forthcoming. Church organisation is in the hands of fallible people, and mistakes and injustices occur. But God knows all, and we should be content with that. It is a difficult but rewarding lesson to learn.

When Robert Morrison went to China with the gospel in 1807 he was allowed to work only outside the walls of Canton. He was permitted to deal only with Chinese merchants. He persevered in learning the language and translating the Bible, but by 1817 he had won only two people for Christ: two converts in ten years! *He* saw little reward, but he surely gained the commendation of his Lord. And that, for him, would be all that mattered.

ENTRUSTED TO US: COMMITTED TO HIM

2 TIMOTHY 1:6–14 – 'I know who it is in whom I have trusted, and am confident of his power to keep safe what he has put into my charge, until the great Day' (v. 12, NEB).

There is an interesting and significant difference in the Authorised Version rendering of the above verse. This says: 'He is able to keep that which *I have committed to him*', whereas the NEB has '. . . *what he has put into my charge*'. The former refers to what the apostle has committed to God, the latter what God has entrusted to him. What did Paul say?

The word translated in the AV as 'that which I have committed' means, literally, 'my deposit', and it could obviously be understood in either of the two ways mentioned. This word appears in two other places in the Timothy letters – in 1 Timothy 6:20 and in 2 Timothy 1:14, and in both cases is rendered in the AV as in the second of the two alternatives – as a deposit committed by God. Therefore we may feel the writer would use the word in the same sense as indicated in the NEB, and that the newer translation is right.

But are not both ideas valid? Had not Paul entrusted himself to God, and not only himself, his 'soul', but also his work, his converts: everything he was and had? And have not we? Like Paul, then, we may be sure that he is able to keep it all safe until the great day when (to use another Pauline phrase) the fight is fought and the course is finished.

It is also true that *God* has entrusted something to *us*. This may be as some suggest 'sound teaching' (v. 13), the true doctrine, the 'faith which was once for all delivered to the saints'. It may also be 'the faith and love which are ours in Christ Jesus' (v. 13). These, too, have been entrusted to us, both to enrich us and also to share with others.

CITIZENS OF HEAVEN AND EARTH

1 PETER 2:11–17 – 'Show proper respect to everyone. Love the brotherhood of believers, fear God, honour the king' (v. 17, NIV).

In recent years there has come a commendable awareness among Christians of the need to be busy about the affairs of this life – a healthy reaction to the once-common idea that all the believer had to bother about was getting himself ready for the next life. One of the popular words among Christians today is *involvement* – and rightly so. So it might be considered that Peter's description of believers as 'aliens and strangers in this world' (v. 11) is out of date.

The truth is that as Christians we should regard ourselves as having an allegiance to 'another world'. We cannot be content to regard ourselves as belonging wholly to this order; there is a spiritual order that transcends it. A description of the Church in the world, written centuries ago in a work called *The Shepherd of Hermas* is always valid: 'They dwell in their own country but only as sojourners; they bear their share in all things as citizens, and they endure all the hardships as strangers. Every foreign country is a fatherland to them, and every fatherland is foreign ... Their existence is on earth, but their citizenship is in heaven.'

Yet Christians cannot opt out of their duties in the world; this Scripture makes this abundantly clear. As Peter says, though Christians are 'aliens and strangers' in the world, God wants them to be 'good citizens' (Jerusalem Bible). Indeed, their faith should help them to make their contribution in a glad, responsible and effective way. It is their knowledge of an eternal dimension that gives quality to all they do on earth.

ADVANTAGE IN ADVERSITY

1 PETER 1:6–12 – 'These have come so that your faith . . . may be proved genuine' (v. 7, NIV).

Nothing is more likely to crush those who are suffering to tell them glibly that pain is 'good for the soul'. Yet it *is* true that suffering may bring enrichment. This is what Peter was endeavouring to impress upon his readers in this passage. Because of their Christian witness they were having to face persecution, either actual or anticipated, and the apostle wanted them to see that their trials could be to their advantage in the purifying of their faith.

It is not an easy matter, even for Christians, to accept that there are advantages in adversity; yet it is a fact that many mature Christian souls have come to their maturity along the road of suffering. One of the characters in a play by Henrik Ibsen asks another, 'Who taught you to sing?', and the answer comes back, 'God sent me sorrow.' Of Jesus himself it is written that 'Son though he was, for him suffering was the way of obedience' (Hebrews 6:8, WB).

This does not mean for us that we should go out of our way to embrace suffering as the *only* way to holiness. It tells us rather that when trials do come unsought – as they surely will – we are to see possibilities for good in them. This is to triumph over our adversity, and to make positive and creative what could, without the grace of God, be negative and destructive. It is to make our thorns into a crown, as Jesus did.

THE PERFECT HUMAN BEING

HEBREWS 4:14–16 – 'For we do not have a high priest who is unable to sympathise with our weaknesses, but we have one who has been tempted in every way – yet was without sin' (v. 15, NIV).

That Jesus came to teach us how to live is undeniable, and is one of the great objectives of the incarnation. Every generation has been desperately short of role models in the art of living, and Jesus provides us with the perfect example. A moment's reflection will persuade us that the way Jesus lived is the way God intends us all to live. We do not have to yield to temptation. Even in the most testing situation we are still well within range of the grace of God. There is no reason why we should succumb.

It helps us to know that Jesus was not immune from temptation, that he was tempted along our ordinary human lines. Following his dramatic temptation in the desert we are told: 'When the devil had finished all this tempting, he left him until an opportune time' (Luke 4:13). That opportunity would soon come.

If sometimes we think our temptations are greater than his because we are less able to fight them, we should remember that his determination not to sin would cause Satan to exert his total power. Perhaps that is a power we have never felt because we yield too easily! Ought we not to resist more?

The verse above makes it clear that Jesus sympathises with our weakness. He understands temptation's power and, although he overcame temptation himself, he does not stand judgmentally over us. He looks upon us lovingly and sympathetically. His perfect understanding makes him the perfect mediator.

HEROIC BAND

HEBREWS 11:32–40 – 'And what more shall I say? I do not have time to tell about Gideon, Barak, Samson, Jephthah, David, Samuel and the prophets, who through faith conquered kingdoms, administered justice, and gained what was promised' (vv. 32,33, NIV).

Moses was the supreme figure in Israel's history. He led the people and communed with God in a unique manner. He was the Law giver, and looked on as the first of the prophets. He brought his wandering, desert tribes right to the Promised Land – even though he never settled there with them.

But the writer to the Hebrews does not simply offer the example of the patriarchs and Moses. He names others, some well known, some less famous. There seems little to link their experiences. They had varying degrees of ability. Their moral character differed. Some were upright, true and noble. Others were downright deceitful and corrupt.

What do they have in common? Faith, certainly, for that is the whole message of this chapter. And something else, too: all faced enormous odds against them. Each at some stage faced a situation which seemed completely hopeless – Gideon with his three hundred, Barak facing chariots, Samson against the Philistines, Jephthah once an outlaw, David against Goliath, Samuel guiding the people, protesting, into an era of kingship.

The message for us is simple. Hebrews teaches us that faith is not something passive, not merely a matter of belief. Faith spurs us on to act for God, even against the odds.

> *Faith, mighty faith, the promise sees,*
> *And looks to that alone;*
> *Laughs at impossibilities*
> *And cries: It shall be done!*
> *Charles Wesley*

CHRISTIAN SOLIDARITY

> 1 JOHN 1:1-4 - 'What we have seen and heard we declare to you, so that you and we together may share in a common life, that life which we share with the Father and his Son Jesus Christ' (v. 3, NEB).

D.T. Niles has pointed out that the religious life has been understood in three ways: as meeting man's daily needs, throwing light upon the mystery of existence, and dealing with man's guilt and wrongdoing. Yet, while these aspects are true for Christian faith they are subordinate. 'The thrust of the Christian message is not primarily about life and its needs, or life and its mystery, or life and its involvement in sin, but about life *and its destiny.*'

So, in this opening passage of John's letter, we find that the unfolding of God's purpose culminates in the Christian fellowship. The manifestation of the life (v. 2), and the declaration of the truth (v. 3), aims at more than the salvation of the individual. It creates a new and distinctive community.

The Greek word (*koinonia*) which is translated 'fellowship' is far richer than any English word can suggest. It indicates partnership in a common cause, joint ownership of common property. Christians 'hold shares together' in the gospel, in suffering, in consolation, in the Holy Spirit, in the coming glory. The sharing of material wealth by the first Christians was simply a spontaneous expression of this deep spiritual reality.

It is in this sense of common ownership that John writes about that 'which we have seen with our eyes'. He himself may well have been an eyewitness of Christ's life, yet this is not the main point he is making. Rather, John is emphasising the solidarity of the Christian community which enables *each* believer to share the 'first-hand-ness' of the Church's total experience.

⇒◆⇐

FREEDOM FROM FEAR

1 JOHN 4:13–21 – 'There is no fear in love; but perfect love casteth out fear' (v. 18, AV).

In Western countries it is traditional to think of Christ as bringing deliverance from sin; but in many parts of Africa, as elsewhere, he comes as a deliverer from fear.

Inhabitants of a Welfare State are unaware of that daily insecurity which grips many of the less fortunate millions. Cheerful souls – all over the world – have no inkling of the feeling of a mind trembling on the cliff-edge of a nervous breakdown. Indeed, fear has to do with 'torment' (v. 18, AV) or, as the NEB says, 'fear brings with it the pains of judgment'. The fearful mind is punished already.

Poor Ama of Akwapim, in Ghana, was convinced she had been turned into a witch. M.J. Field wrote of her, 'She has spent the last eleven years in travelling round from one medicine man to another . . . She has herself spent on her illness more than £350 of her cocoa fortune.' In Britain, no doubt, she would have seen numerous psychiatrists.

'He first loved us' – to grasp this truth is the first step to deliverance. Courage is the conquest, not the absence, of fear. 'I can't but *I must*', muttered sixteen-year-old Kate Lee as she stood on the step of a Wood Green, London, public house with a bundle of copies of *The War Cry* under her arm . . . white and shaking she made her way in. It was always like that for her. When she died Harold Begbie wrote, 'There is no hope for the world until the love that was in Kate Lee is in us.'

Part 9

UNIVERSAL,
TRIUMPHANT GOSPEL

In this final section the focus is on two short books from the Old Testament, Ruth and Jonah, and also on part of a long book from the New, the Revelation of John. But what, it may well be asked, have these in common that justifies their being placed together like this? Ruth and Jonah certainly have a similar theme, though approached in quite different ways. Their powerful message is, put briefly: God's love and mercy extend to people of all races: none is outside his care and control.

Ruth was possibly written as a protest against the rigid marriage laws imposed by Ezra following the Babylonian exile. Some Jews had married foreigners, and in Ezra's eyes that threatened the purity of God's people. So he ordered all Jewish males to divorce their foreign wives. But this charming tale gently points out that even David, their great and ideal king, was descended from a foreigner, the Moabite woman Ruth.

In its own way the book of Jonah makes a similar point. The prophet was told to go and preach to the Ninevites – of all people! They were known everywhere for their cruelty and oppression. The Jews had suffered at their hands, and another prophet, Nahum, fulminates against them in no uncertain manner. So Jonah refuses to go. When, given a second chance, he *does* go he finds that this wicked, hated people receive the message and repent. Even *they* were capable of that! The lesson is plain: God loves all; and all people everywhere have the potential to respond to God's message and repent.

With its strong message of the final victory of Christ, the Revelation of John underlines all that. It says that God is in control of history (all nations!), and its testimony to the ultimate triumph of right is unsurpassed in the New Testament. Revelation is a difficult (and consequently much-neglected) book; all its treasures are not on the surface by any means. But prayerful consideration of the underlying principles of the book will give us confidence to meet the challenges and changes of the times in which we live.

The comments chosen here from Revelation centre on the first three chapters, where John addresses seven churches. The comments on Ruth and Jonah cover the whole of these two brief books.

AGAINST PREJUDICE

RUTH 1:1–7 – 'Elimelech, Naomi's husband, died, and she was left with her two sons. They married Moabite women, one named Orpah and the other Ruth' (vv. 3,4, NIV).

To understand this simple but delightful tale, we must recall the situation in Judah after the Jews returned from Exile. They were striving to re-establish their national life around temple worship and devotion to the Law. Intermarriage with people of surrounding nations had become common and this was seen by some as a threat to the integrity of the Jewish faith. Ezra, the religious reformer, compelled Jewish males to divorce their non-Jewish wives. We can well imagine the opposition this provoked, and it could have been that this ancient story was applied to this deeply personal controversy. The heroine of this story was more likely to soften hard hearts than any amount of argument, particularly as this Moabite woman was the great-grandmother of Israel's ideal king, David.

Perhaps the writer had already discovered how immune to reasonable argument is racial prejudice. Christian psychiatrist David Stafford-Clark pointed out that racial prejudice and certain forms of mental illness have much in common. 'Prejudice is as mercilessly necessary and as morally corrosive to the prejudiced man, as alcohol is to the alcoholic . . . prejudice is a drug of addiction; and like every other object of addiction . . . it becomes indispensable to the addicted subject . . . the thing that makes him feel worth while; take it away and he is unbearably distressed and diminished.'

Even if we are free from *racial* prejudice, there may well be other areas in which we have a compulsive need to feel superior. A prayer: 'Jesus, Saviour of human activity to which you have given meaning . . . be also the Saviour of human unity; compel us to discard our pettiness and to venture forth, resting on you, into the undaunted ocean of charity' (Pierre Teilhard de Chardin).

THE HEART HAS ITS REASONS

RUTH 1:8–14 – ' "Return home, my daughters, I am too old to have another husband" ' (v. 12, NIV).

When a married man died in the ancient East, it was customary for his brother to marry the widow. This ensured that the widow kept her place in society and did not remain childless. It is to this custom, which was also incorporated in the law of Deuteronomy (25:5–10), that Naomi referred when trying to persuade her two daughters-in-law to return to their own homes. Even if she married again immediately, argues Naomi, they could hardly wait until she had reared more sons for them. The logic was irrefutable, but Ruth was not to be deterred.

Perhaps we should allow this moving story to remind us that intuition, feelings and emotions are as important as intellect. Ideally, mind and heart should be *equal* partners. E.N. Ducker describes a young man whose mother trained him solely by reasoned argument, instinctual responses being almost entirely suppressed. The result was that decisions which most people would make intuitively, and with a minimum of stress, were subjected by this young man to exhaustive analysis. He even worked out a series of logical tests, which required at least three months to complete, in order that, when he met a girl, he could assess her suitability for him. A one-sided emphasis upon the importance of the intellect had made him an emotional cripple!

If we have sometimes talked in a rather superior way about 'mere' emotion, perhaps we need to think again.

AGE-OLD PROBLEM

RUTH 1:15–22 – ' "I went away full, but the Lord has brought me back empty" ' (v. 21, NIV).

Almost as eloquent as Ruth's protest of undying loyalty is Naomi's declaration of her profound sorrow: 'Don't call me Naomi [pleasant] any more . . . Call me Mara [bitter], because the Almighty has made my life very bitter.' What are we to make of this view that God is responsible for human ills and suffering?

In the Bible the problem of evil is faced in two ways which appear contradictory. First, it is affirmed that God is ultimately responsible for everything, for there is no other being of equal power. The Jews rejected dualism, the belief in two rival, independent gods, one good and one evil. Second, the Bible claims that God is wholly good and is utterly opposed to all sin, disease and evil.

Logically, these assertions do not harmonise, but since evil is an insoluble mystery this need not surprise us. Both are equally important for, as John Hick says, we need both to recognise the crucial antagonism between good and evil and yet to know that only good possesses finality. 'Experienced from within the stresses of human existence, evil *is* a sheerly malevolent reality, hostile alike to God and his creation. It is a threat to be feared, a temptation to be resisted, a foe to be fought.' At the same time we need to be able to look up and assert God's sovereign control over evil. Neither its beginning, its course, nor its end lies outside God's ultimate control.

VIVID IMAGERY

RUTH 2:1–12 – ' "May you be richly rewarded by the Lord, the God of Israel, under whose wings you have come to take refuge" ' (v. 12, NIV).

Those who live amid the towering concrete and noisy bustle of modern cities find the story of Ruth gleaning in the harvest field full of natural charm. Yet this is more than a picture of rural simplicity. The custom of leaving some sheaves for the poor to collect was established in Israel's law and specifically linked with the kindness of God himself (Deuteronomy 24:18–22).

In those days it was taken for granted that anyone going to live in a foreign country would transfer his allegiance to that nation's god. This is reflected in the words of Boaz to Ruth. We notice the vivid pictorial language used about God. In the first chapter Naomi spoke of 'the Lord's hand' (v. 13); here Boaz says that Ruth has sought shelter under the 'wings' of God.

It is surely a mark of misplaced sophistication to imagine that in thinking about God we can dispense with rich poetic imagery like that of the Bible. Translate this imagery into abstract theological terms and see how lifeless it becomes. Our great need today is to discover fresh imagery drawn from the contemporary world. Unfortunately, the impersonal nature of much modern life makes this difficult. But while fresh images are sought we would be unwise to condemn ourselves to live in a desert of abstraction. It is a mistake to imagine that doctrinal definitions convey more of the reality of God than poetic images. And, of course, it is equally mistaken to think that either abstractions or images convey the *whole* of God.

LOVE IN ACTION

RUTH 2:17–23 – '"The Lord bless him!" Naomi said to her daughter-in-law. "The Lord has not stopped showing kindness to the living and the dead"' (v. 20, NIV).

'Be kind,' exhorted the great French preacher Lacordaire, 'it is so like God!' The kindness of Boaz to Ruth seems to mark the turning point in this story. Before this all is tragedy, even though the gloom is somewhat lightened by Ruth's unswerving affection and loyalty. Now, however, Naomi is reassured of the goodness of the divine providence by the generosity of a man.

Kindness has been called 'love in action' and we do well to test the genuineness of our love, which we can mistakenly assess in terms of emotion, by its concrete expression. 'Love may mean writing with enough care so that our correspondence can be read without spending time deciphering; that is, it may mean taking the time to save his time. To love is to pay one's bills; it is to keep things in order so that the wife's work will be made easier. It means arriving somewhere on time; it means giving your full attention to the one who is talking to you. To miss what he says means we are more interested in what we are telling ourselves inwardly than in what he is telling us' (Paul Tournier).

Can such small matters reassure another of so great a truth as the goodness of God? Our story, and a good deal of human experience, suggest that they can.

SEEKING A REDEEMER

RUTH 3:1–10 – ' "I am your servant Ruth," she said, "Spread the corner of your garment over me, since you are a kinsman-redeemer" ' (v. 9, NIV).

The next-of-kin male of an Israelite family was under obligation to take up the case of any relative who fell upon bad times. He was called the 'kinsman' and the Hebrew word for it is frequently translated 'redeemer'. If a man was unlucky, fell into debt, and was forced to sell his land then it was the duty of the kinsman to 'redeem' or 'ransom' it, to buy it back, and to re-establish his relative. In doing this the kinsman was acting on behalf of God to whom all Israel's land belonged.

Boaz was related to Naomi and in this episode of the story she is hoping that he will play the part of the kinsman by marrying Ruth. The writer of this book was the first to include such marriage among the obligations of the kinsman. What is even more startling, 'Naomi is seeking to make Boaz act for God as the redeemer of an alien woman who is legally outside the redeemed community, God's chosen people Israel' (George Knight). This simple love story was probably theological dynamite when first written!

In his book, *The Bible Doctrine of Salvation*, C. Ryder Smith expressed the wish that there were some such English verb as 'to kinsman'. This would certainly help us to see the sacrifice of Jesus in a new and vivid way, for the idea of the kinsman lies behind the words of Jesus about giving his life as a 'ransom' for many.

SPIRIT AND MATTER

RUTH 4:1–7 – ' "I cannot redeem it because I might endanger my own estate. You redeem it yourself. I cannot do it" ' (v. 6, NIV).

Although Boaz was willing to play the part of the kinsman by marrying Ruth and redeeming the land that belonged to her dead husband, there was a nearer relative who had prior claim to play this role. Therefore, this man was first given the opportunity, but it was made clear to him that both the dead man's land and his widow must be redeemed. When he protested that such a purchase would leave him insufficient capital to hand to his own sons the way was clear for Boaz to marry Ruth.

This strange bargaining, so remote from our modern thinking, is yet closely related to one fundamental biblical truth – the inseparable relationship between spirit and matter. 'Ruth the person cannot be redeemed unless her property is redeemed along with her . . . Ruth's redemption implies the redemption of all she has' (George Knight).

When an unChristian wedge is driven between soul and body, spirit and matter, then religion becomes irrelevant and useless. The Salvation Army has tried to express this truth in its dual emphasis upon proclaiming the gospel and social service. 'They are but two activities of the one and the same salvation which is concerned with the total redemption of man. Both rely on the same divine grace. Both are inspired by the same motive. Both have the same end in mind. And as the gospel has joined them together we do not propose to put them asunder,' said Frederick Coutts, one-time international leader of the Salvation Army.

The same integrity of concern for the whole man should also be expressed in our everyday relationships.

MORE THAN A HAPPY ENDING

RUTH 4:13–17 – 'And they named him Obed. He was the father of Jesse, the father of David' (v. 17, NIV).

Taken out of the context in which it was written, the book of Ruth reads like a delightful but not very significant love story. Is it more than a tale about kindly people with a happy-ever-after ending? If we place it in the post-exilic period, when the Jewish nation was trying to thrash out the problem of its relationship with the Gentile world, the homely narrative becomes a powerful argument. If King David himself was descended from a Moabite woman, nationalistic intolerance was surely out of the question. There were, of course, strong historical reasons why Judah should remain distinct from surrounding nations, yet this necessity easily became an excuse for harshness, prejudice and an imagined superiority.

The abiding value of this book is in its warning against prejudice. Søren Kierkegaard suggested that a fixed idea is like cramp in the foot – the best cure is to stamp on it! F.W. Boreham once bought thirty-six books in a bundle at an auction; six he wanted and thirty he didn't. Yet among the thirty he found so much of value that he learnt how important it is to disregard one's initial reaction. 'If I hold to one opinion,' he wrote, 'I must studiously cultivate the acquaintance of men who hold the opposite view, and investigate the hidden recesses of their minds.'

If this is true in the realm of ideas, how much more important it is that we should practise the same openness in regard to people.

CONCERN FOR THE DESPICABLE?

JONAH 1:1–6 – 'The word of the Lord came to Jonah . . .
"Go to the great city of Nineveh and preach against it . . ."
But Jonah ran away from the Lord and headed for Tarshish.
After paying his fare, he went aboard' (vv. 1,2,3, NIV).

The story of Jonah begins in traditional prophetic style: 'The word
of the Lord came . . .' But what follows is unlike any other prophetic
book in that it consists of the story of Jonah's experiences, and
displays all the characteristics of a parable or, better, an allegory.
It is widely assumed that Jonah is intended as a symbol for Israel
and that the message of the book is a message for the Jews.

'Go to Nineveh!' That command was a repulsive prospect to a
Jew; most of them would have done exactly what Jonah did, run
as far away as they could in the other direction! As far as the Jews
were concerned, Nineveh was, and always had been, associated with
extreme evil and cruelty. Another of the Hebrew prophets said about
the destruction of the city: 'All who have heard of your fate clap
their hands in joy. Are there any whom your ceaseless cruelty has
not borne down?' (Nahum 3:19).

Why should God be concerned with such despicable people? The
Jews were intended to discover that their God was a God with a
missionary heart and that Nineveh was part of his concern. But
Jonah acts out his defiance of God's command and sets out for
Tarshish.

We can hardly miss the parallel between the command given to
Jonah and that given to the Church. Is our obedience any better
than his? We don't have to run away to act out our unwillingness
to obey; we have only to sit entrenched in our comfort. There is
a constant need for us to be reminded that God's love embraces
all mankind, and his servants must not be reluctant to share in
declaring that truth.

UNIVERSAL, TRIUMPHANT GOSPEL

'THE BLUFF OF WEAKNESS'

JONAH 1:4–16 – 'But the Lord let loose a hurricane, and the
sea ran so high in the storm that the ship threatened to break
up' (v. 4, NEB).

This passage – descriptive writing of high quality – makes two
important points. Firstly, the initiative is always with God. It is
he who creates the storm to teach Jonah a lesson he will not soon
forget. Though we are moral, responsible beings with freedom
of choice, we must not forget that in the last resort we are in
God's hands.

Wrote J.B. Phillips, 'You and I only live because God has given
us life. We use bodies and minds and faculties which we had no
hand in designing. We live in a world which we had no part in
creating . . . So, although it remains true that God will never force
our hands or overpower our wills, yet this is his world in which
we live and move and have our being. In that sense God is quite
inescapable.' This is a truth both sobering and heartening.

This reading also emphasises something the Jews would receive
with little pleasure – that all the good people were not in Israel. The
Gentile sailors were kindly, generous men who made every effort to
avoid having to throw Jonah overboard although in their eyes he
was clearly responsible for their plight. And they also responded
to the true God when he was made known to them (v. 16). What
a rebuke to bigoted Israelites!

About bigotry, a divisive, evil thing, A.D. Martin wrote, 'It is
always the brazen front of misgiving, it is the bluff of weakness,
the bloat of the flesh which reveals anaemia in the blood.' People of
stubborn prejudices regarding their own circle, their religious group,
should carefully consider these words. It might even be salutary to
apply them to ourselves!

'SALVATION COMES FROM THE LORD'

JONAH 2:1–10 – 'From deep inside the fish Jonah prayed' (v. 1, GNB).

The story of Jonah is interrupted by a psalm of thanksgiving – verses 2 to 9 – which is regarded as a masterly example of Hebrew poetry. But it fits uneasily into the rest of the book. Jonah does not emerge from the narrative sections as the creature given to gratitude and thanksgiving which this psalm suggests. This misfit has caused most scholars to regard the psalm as a piece of poetry which has been imported into the book, probably by a writer, or maybe a later editor, as an expression of the prayer mentioned in verse 1, and to make a theological point about salvation (v. 9).

It is in this context of salvation that the psalm and its use are best understood. If we look again at the experience of Jonah we notice that the point at which he was saved was at 1:17. It was not the large fish that threatened Jonah's existence but the watery grave. His subsequent deliverance on the beach, described in 2:10, was the outcome of a saving act. In a sense, then, the psalm sums up the whole story of Jonah and expounds the story of divine grace.

Leslie C. Allen has written, 'The psalm plays its part in demonstrating an overall theme depicting the inconsistency of one graciously brought back from the brink of deserved destruction churlishly resenting the divine right to rescue other sinners from perishing.' Christian thanksgiving for grace received has to be seen in grace proclaimed, or the Church also sinks into churlishness.

BACK TO 'SQUARE ONE'

JONAH 3:1–4 – 'The word of the Lord came to Jonah a second time: "Go to the great city of Nineveh, go now and denounce it in the words I give you"' (vv. 1,2, NEB).

Jonah's salvation did not include an escape from his responsibilities before God. Notice how the verses of 3:1,2 echo 1:1,2 and bring Jonah back to his original commission. His earlier experience had wrought sufficient change in him to cause him to obey without resistance or argument. Jonah sets out for Nineveh and declares God's judgment to the people (v. 4).

This part of the Jonah narrative highlights an essential spiritual principle. It is true of course that not every rebellious sinner is able to get back to 'square one'. The passage of years and developing circumstances often make it impossible to take up the actual task that was earlier rejected, and in that sense we don't all get Jonah's chance. Any spiritual regeneration requires that we face the basic issue of obedience to God. It may be impossible to accept the original commission but the issue then becomes: Will you, as one redeemed, accept each *new* commission in true obedience?

God does not run out of alternatives when we are truly penitent, but he is not a God of the soft option. His salvation offers no escape from the basic responsibility to be obedient. He has to bring us back again and again to face that fundamental issue until we, like Jonah, respond positively.

REPENTANT HEATHEN?

JONAH 3:5–10 – 'The people of Nineveh believed God's word. They ordered a public fast and put on sackcloth' (v. 5, NEB).

It comes as a surprise when people who have been regarded as beyond the pale react in a thoroughly normal manner. That the barbarians of Nineveh responded to God's message of impending destruction with a thoroughgoing repentance must have come as a shock to those Jews who first heard or read the story of Jonah. The expression of repentance is so typically Jewish as to be almost unbelievable. Sackcloth, ashes and fasting were Jewish expressions. At Nineveh it is described as affecting the people (v. 5), the king (v. 6) and the official life of the nation (vv. 7,8). Even the animals were to be included. There was also a call to prayer and to an amendment of life. This was to be no mere ceremonial repentance.

Could such actions secure a reprieve for a people like the Ninevites? The king there did not presume that repentance *earned* deliverance, as the term 'it may be' in verse 9 shows. At this point in the story the writer leaves his readers with the hint that the salvation of the Ninevites is a possibility, but it is doubtful if many Jews of that time would have entertained the prospect.

Is it possible for us Christians sometimes to look at today's unbelievers with such narrow-minded prejudice?

BETRAYED

JONAH 4:1–3 – 'Jonah was very unhappy . . . So he prayed,
"Lord, didn't I say before I left home that this is just what
you would do? . . . Now, Lord, let me die. I am better off
dead than alive"' (vv. 1,2,3, GNB).

Jonah could try to run away from God; he could sleep through a
storm (1:5); he could face death by drowning (1:12); he could be
rescued by what must have been a most frightening means (1:17)
– but he could *not* live with the idea that God had forgiven the
Ninevites. Although he claimed that he knew from the beginning
that 'God was merciful, slow to anger, and abounding in steadfast
love' (v. 2, RSV), Jonah felt betrayed because God had not destroyed
Nineveh and the Ninevites.

You might suppose that someone so recently saved from a fate
that he deserved would be glad to see others saved – but not
Jonah. He was resentful of God's love being shown to the people
he disapproved of. He had not really learned much about the God
he claimed to know so well. He was looking for a God in his own
image, and instead of being terrified by that prospect he would
rather die than admit that he was wrong.

The book has a remarkable capacity to touch a very sensitive
nerve in our Christian work. It is the universal message of salvation
that gives purpose to our mission. If we lose the conviction that *all
people* are the objects of God's care, we lose the sense of urgency
in our evangelism.

NO RIGHT AT ALL

JONAH 4:4–11 – ' "Have you any right to be angry?" ' (v. 4, NIV).

The question at the beginning of this reading is, says Peter Ackroyd in a brief but perceptive commentary on the little book, the one sentence in the whole story in which its message is summed up: 'Have you any right to be angry?' Of course Jonah had no right at all to be angry because God bestows forgiveness on people of other races who truly repent. And the Jewish nation had no right to stand aloof from others, considering them to have no claim on God's favour.

And we Christians – the New Israel – have no right to sit back and complacently imagine we have discharged our duty when we have said our prayers, worshipped on Sunday and made a contribution to overseas missions or some evangelistic campaign.

We cannot read the book of Jonah and avoid its call to the whole Church to engage in bringing others to Christ. To quote George A.F. Knight: 'The responsibility of being a Christian is appalling. The Christian is called not primarily to lead the good life, not to rejoice in a self-conscious faith, not even to engage in a search for holy living. The latter may turn out to be the ultimate form of selfishness. The Christian is called to obedience, utter obedience to the voice of God. And it is as he obeys that goodness, faith and holiness come to him.'

This modern writer points out that in the last judgment it will not be Nineveh alone that will be sternly appraised by God, so will Israel – that is ourselves as Christians – because the responsibility of telling Nineveh has been laid upon us. This the book of Jonah makes abundantly clear.

MESSAGE OF HOPE

REVELATION 1:1–3 – 'John . . . testifies to everything he saw – that is, the word of God and the testimony of Jesus Christ' (v. 2, NIV).

In the opening verses of the Prologue to this great book, the writer says clearly that the source of his message is God himself. This message was given through Jesus Christ, who sent his angel to his servant John. It has, therefore, divine authority.

Let us pause just now on the thought that as committed Christians we *all* have a responsibility for passing on a message which has its source in God, and that it is in essence the message of this book: that God in Christ has conquered evil; that however great the present confusion and the temptation to doubt and despair, the ultimate triumph of the good is assured. Our message, like John's, is supremely a message of hope.

In his book *Period of My Life*, F.R. Barry wrote on 'the tragic dimension in human history', thinking, he said, that 'the present civilisation may collapse and go down in a horror of anarchy and blood'. There are, he affirmed, strong reasons for fear but continued, 'there are stronger reasons for hope. I have hope for the future in which our grandchildren will grow up because I believe in God and the providential government of history. I believe that God raised Jesus from the dead and committed himself to the cause of Christ as his own cause. Good, yet undreamed of, is within man's reach if he has the courage and faith to take it.'

The writer's *if* suggests something we might well ponder. Have we that kind of courage and faith?

GOD IN CONTROL

REVELATION 1:4–8 – ' "I am the Alpha and the Omega," says the Lord God, "who is, and who was, and who is to come, the Almighty" ' (v. 8, NIV).

The number seven was a Jewish symbol of completeness, and in writing to seven churches John was in fact addressing himself to the whole Church. His message is for us! What does he say, then, in these magnificent verses? He declares his testimony to the greatness of the love and power of God. The three-fold blessing (vv. 4,5) is followed by a doxology to Jesus Christ through whom, the writer is fully convinced, God has done all things. He has shown his love, secured man's salvation and established his own kingdom. And the future is not in doubt, since Christ 'is coming with the clouds'.

This expression emphasises a truth the persecuted Christians in that day desperately needed to hear and grasp, and which God through his messenger explicitly states, that 'God holds all things in control' (v. 8, Barclay). Whatever is happening to them now, however strongly the power of pagan Rome was directed against them, God's ultimate purpose could not be defeated since he is the timeless one, 'who is and who was and who is to come'.

Perhaps a large part of our trouble today is that we have a pitifully restricted view of God's purpose; we are near-sighted and fail so often to estimate the present against the large canvas of history, which is under God's direction. J.B. Phillips wrote a book with the title, *Your God is Too Small*, in which he adequately described the fault of too many of us. Faith in a bigger God, a God of mighty purpose (of which we are a part) will fortify us in our present, temporary, trials.

USING OUR AFFLICTIONS

REVELATION 1:9–11 – 'I, John . . . was on the island of Patmos because of the word of God and the testimony of Jesus' (v. 9, NIV).

Patmos was a small rocky island off the coast of Asia Minor, about seventy-five miles from Ephesus, to which John was banished because he had proclaimed God's word and publicly declared his faith in Jesus Christ. This probably meant that he had refused to participate in the Emperor-worship that was made compulsory towards the end of the first century AD. But though he was banished from home and friends he could not be separated from God, an experience shared by many of Christ's followers.

The seventeenth-century mystic Madame Guyon wrote a number of hymns in prison where she was held because of her religious views. These hymns include 'All scenes alike engaging prove', one verse of which has the lines:

> *My love! How full of sweet content*
> *I pass my years in banishment.*

Like John with his visions and Madame Guyon with her hymns, many Christians, some well known and others obscure, have learned to turn their afflictions into creative achievements. The point to notice here is that these people did not simply *endure* their hardships, holding on *in spite of them* – which is, of course, commendable – they *used them* to good effect.

It is not easy to learn to do this, for even devout Christians are not exempt from the temptation to indulgent self-pity when trials come. Jesus himself, with his cross of suffering and shame, supremely illustrates the glory of taking a seemingly impossible situation and using it to the blessing of others. It is only those who learn of him who begin to make progress along this difficult but not impossible way.

CHRIST IN THE MIDST

REVELATION 1:12–20 – 'When I turned I saw seven golden lampstands, and among the lampstands was someone like a son of man' (vv. 12,13, NIV).

John's expression, 'someone like a son of man' recalls Daniel 7:13, where one of that description was given sovereignty, glory and kingly power. Also, the term was the one most often used by Jesus in reference to himself. Here the words clearly refer to the Risen Christ; and while it may not be possible to ascertain the significance of every detail of his appearance, some characteristics of Christ are suggested. His wisdom is portrayed by his snow-white hair; that he is a discerning judge is indicated by the eyes that flame like fire; that he is triumphant over his enemies is noted by his feet which gleam like burnished brass.

It is important to notice where the Son of man stood – 'among the lampstands'. As the lampstands represent the seven churches (v. 20) – that is, the whole Church – the meaning is that Christ stands now and for ever among his people. 'The Church . . . is in the midst of conflict and woe, but the Son of Man is in the midst of the Church' (J.P. Love) – a heartening thought.

The fear John felt at seeing the imposing figure was unnecessary, for while there was a certain terrible majesty about him, he spoke words of comfort. 'Do not be afraid,' he said. 'I am the First and the Last' – that is, the Ever-present One. Furthermore, he had conquered death: 'I was dead, and behold I am alive for ever and ever.'

These are eternal truths; their message is for Christ's Church to the end of time. That we have not sufficiently grasped them may explain much of our present-day fear and doubt.

'THE GREATEST OF THESE'

REVELATION 2:1–7 – 'You have persevered and have endured hardships for my name, and have not grown weary. Yet I hold this against you: You have forsaken your first love' (vv. 3,4, NIV).

The first message is addressed to the Christians at Ephesus, the chief city of Asia Minor, where the church had become one of the foremost centres of the Christian faith. Christ knew all their ways, which meant, for one thing, that he was aware of their good qualities. They had exhibited patient endurance as they worked in Christ's cause. Zealous for the purity of the faith, they had toiled hard in resisting and overcoming false teaching. Yet, despite all this, they received the condemnation of Christ because *their love had waned.*

We cannot be sure whether this meant their love for Christ himself or, as Moffatt's translation of the phrase suggests, their love for each other. In the welter of controversy over the vigorous defence of truth, both are possible. But the point is unimportant, for love for God and love for other people can hardly be separated. What should be noted carefully is that without love even zeal for the truth is of little worth.

This is something Christian people have not always remembered, and we do not have to go back to the days of the inquisition to see it! It is important that none of us forgets, as Paul puts it, that 'the greatest of these is love'. Christ's invitation to the Ephesian Christian was: 'Remember ... repent ... do' – three parts of one total response, answering to the 'three stages in the history of conversion' (H.B. Swete). Those who go back on their first love are in a sad and perilous position, and to ignore Christ's invitation leads to disaster. Yet how wonderfully possible is the way of renewal and restoration!

TRUE RICHES

REVELATION 2:8–11 – 'I know how hard pressed you are, and poor – and yet you are rich!' (v. 9, NEB).

Smyrna, a rich and prosperous city and strong ally of Rome, had a large Jewish population. This meant it was a particularly dangerous place in which to be a Christian, for the Jews were strongly opposed to the Christian faith and eagerly assisted the Roman authorities in their persecution of those who followed Christ's way. To the Christians of this place Christ spoke words of commendation. He knew how materially poor they were, and how bitterly they were being persecuted. Yet, he said, they were truly rich, rich in faith and love.

This underlines the truth that material poverty and, indeed, poverty of intellectual endowment and education, need not be barriers to *spiritual* wealth.

Leslie Brown, one-time Bishop of Edmundsbury and Ipswich, tells of an old lady who lived over a bookmaker's shop when he, the Bishop, was a curate at Portsmouth. He knew her in her last days when she was confined to bed in her room. All the curates of the parish used to visit this saintly woman when they were depressed. The Bishop says he remembered going to her room one day and she said – this funny little, old, illiterate woman who had never been to school, and who was lying in bed, alone, with a broken leg – 'Oh, Mr Brown, I am so delighted to see you! I was just thinking *what would we do without the Holy Spirit?*'

While not despising the blessings money may bring, or repudiating the benefits of a good education, Christians recognise that real success is to be estimated only in what they know of God, and in how truly they follow in his way.

WHEN TOLERANCE IS A MISTAKE

REVELATION 2:12–17 – 'I know where you live – where Satan has his throne. Yet you remain true to my name. You did not renounce your faith in me' (v. 13, NIV).

The third church to be addressed was at Pergamum, a strong centre of pagan worship. The city had a temple dedicated to the worship of the Roman emperor. The god of healing, Asclepius, whose symbol was a serpent (to the Christians the symbol of Satan) was commonly worshipped there. Furthermore, on a hill outside the city there were any number of heathen temples. John calls the city the place where 'Satan has his throne' – and no wonder! Yet the Christians had resisted the pressures and not denied their faith.

Their example is a rebuke to those who lament that the peculiar difficulties where they live and work make it impossible to maintain an effective witness. That the Pergamum Christians succeeded knocks away any excuses of that kind.

However, having resisted so remarkably the dangers from *without* the church, they had not been so successful with the perils *within*. Christ's indictment of them was that they tolerated too passively the false teaching of some of their number, and had been seduced to idolatrous practices, as Balaam had seduced Israel from the way of truth (a reference to an Old Testament incident recorded in Numbers 31:16).

G.B. Caird remarked that 'the fault of Pergamum is the opposite of the fault of Ephesus' (whose intolerance of others was reflected in their waning love) and continued, 'How narrow is the safe path between the sin of tolerance and the sin of intolerance'.

Where do we draw the line? Where in fact does the safe path lie? The questions provide food for thought.

PRAISE AND BLAME

REVELATION 2:18–29 – 'I know your deeds, your love and faith, your service and perseverance . . . Nevertheless, I have this against you' (vv. 19,20, NIV).

Praise of a high order was given to the Christians of Thyatira. They were full of love and faithfulness, and were zealous in good works; they had remained steadfast under difficulties and were making progress in Christian life and service. Unlike the Ephesians, who were criticised for losing their first love, the Thyatirans were doing better than ever they had done. Such commendation indicated a Christian community of high quality. However, there was the sobering 'Yet . . .' Notwithstanding so many good points, the life of the church was being marred by certain unhappy factors.

Some of the members had allowed themselves to be influenced away from sound doctrine and worthy practices. The name Jezebel probably only symbolised a party or an individual (maybe a woman) who was encouraging some form of debased worship as, in the time of Ahab, Queen Jezebel had introduced the false god Baal to Israel (1 Kings 16:19–34). Such a situation in Thyatira had to be severely condemned as the Christians there were strongly urged to hold fast to what they had been taught.

This sad state of affairs emphasises the possibility of wrong thinking and wrong practices becoming, almost imperceptibly, an established part of the life of God's people; of the Church getting so accustomed to evil in the midst that it is no longer seen for what it is. This is a danger into which the individual Christian may also fall. The only safeguard is by prayer and meditation to seek the guiding light of the Holy Spirit. He, in love, both reveals our errors and leads us into truth.

WORKING AT OUR FAITH

REVELATION 3:1–6 – 'Wake up! Strengthen what remains and is about to die, for I have not found your deeds complete in the sight of God' (v. 2, NIV).

Twice in the history of Sardis the undisciplined living, love of luxury and licentiousness of its inhabitants had proved the city's undoing. Although it had good natural fortification, lack of vigilance in the defenders had resulted in its capture on two separate occasions, the attackers in each case climbing the hill on which the city was built to make their way unobserved and unchecked.

Now, writes John, the Christians of the city are guilty of that very error in respect to the faith, and he calls them to wake up for, as D.T. Niles paraphrased it, 'your very lack of watchfulness will be your complete undoing'. That the church at Sardis had a reputation for vigour was true enough, but it was really dead.

Christians cannot afford to drift into a state of half-heartedness about their faith and life, as those at Sardis had done. John exhorted them to *remember* and *repent*. Let them look back to the days when they had been obedient and full of faith, he said in effect; let them turn from their neglect and embrace the cause of Christ enthusiastically.

This speaks to us all of the necessity for *conscious effort* in the development of Christian character. As Paul points out, we have to 'work . . . at our salvation' (Philippians 2:12, JM). Do we put into our spiritual life the disciplined effort we put into, say, our careers? Dietrich Bonhoeffer wrote: 'Our relationship with God must be practised . . . Religion means work, and perhaps the hardest and certainly the holiest work a man can undertake.'

OPPORTUNITIES TO SERVE

REVELATION 3:7–13 – 'I have placed before you an open door that no-one can shut' (v. 8, NIV).

The church at Philadelphia (the name means 'brotherly love') was small and poor, yet John had nothing but praise for the believers there. They were proving faithful, despite the hostility of the Jews or, as John puts it 'who claim to be Jews'. By this he meant that those Jews who had rejected the Christian revelation had forfeited their right to be called the chosen of God. They who acknowledged Christ as Lord were the true children of Abraham.

Notice the promised reward for faithfulness – *greater opportunities for service*. Christ had set before them 'an open door'. Philadelphia was founded as a centre for the spread of Greek culture; now the Christians of that same city would have the inestimable privilege of making their church a centre for the spread of the Christian message.

The door of opportunity, opened to all who follow Christ, is a door which no one can shut. We might remember this truth when we are tempted to feel that our circumstances debar us from making an effective witness. Obviously, the conditions of our life may *limit* our opportunities, but they can never *shut the door*; only our unfaithfulness can do that.

Many Christians have found that adverse circumstances have led to even larger ways of serving Christ, like Paul with his imprisonment. He wrote, 'What has happened to me has really served to advance the gospel' (Philippians 1:12). Opportunities to serve are before us. Our need is for the vision to see and the courage to grasp them.

THE LIVING FLAME

REVELATION 3:14–22 – 'You say, "I am rich . . ." but you do not realise that you are wretched, pitiful, poor, blind and naked' (v. 17, NIV).

Laodicea, a rich and prosperous city, was a banking centre and also produced a special kind of black cloth and a well-known eye-salve. There are allusions to this in verse 17 where the believers were exhorted to seek 'gold refined in the fire' (with all the dross removed); and *white* clothes to wear; not the local eye-salve, but that which will allow them to see *spiritually*. The truth was that for all the material prosperity of the city, in which the Christians doubtless shared, the church was spiritually poor and, what was worse, indifferent to its condition.

Self-sufficiency and indifference are faults to which prosperous religious people are particularly vulnerable – a truth to which Jesus himself drew attention. Christian experience commences and continues in a realistic awareness of need, a recognition that we are not self-sufficient. Frederich Schleiermacher, the nineteenth-century theologian, defined religion as 'a feeling of absolute dependence', a concept supported throughout the Bible. Life is impossible without God, and indifference is not only the death of spiritual life but also a sure brake on the progress of Christ's cause in the world.

How enthusiastically do we hold the truth we have received? How zealously do we guard and propagate our faith? Sound argument and appeal to reason are valuable and necessary, and the wise evangelist will not spurn them; but, as J.S. Stewart said, 'Precision and logic are bought too dear if they stifle the living flame.'